New Interpretations
of Aboriginal American Culture
History

75th Anniversary
Volume
of the
Anthropological Society
of Washington

NEW YORK
COOPER SQUARE PUBLISHERS, INC.
1972

Originally Published, 1955
Published 1972 by Cooper Square Publishers, Inc.
59 Fourth Avenue, New York, N. Y. 10003
International Standard Book No. 0-8154-0419-0
Library of Congress Catalog Card No. 72-78236

Printed in U.S.A. by
NOBLE OFFSET PRINTERS, INC.
New York, N.Y. 10003

TABLE OF CONTENTS

LIST OF FIGURES

LIST OF TABLES

ACKNOWLEDGEMENTS

Grateful acknowledgement is made to the following publishers for permission to reproduce excerpts in the paper, *The Coming of Age of American Archeology* by B. J. Meggers:

CAMBRIDGE UNIVERSITY PRESS
   Eddington, A. S.: *The Nature of the Physical World,* 1928.
   Jeans, James: *Physics and Philosophy,* 1943.
McGRAW-HILL BOOK CO., INC.
   Hoebel, E. A.: *Man in the Primitive World,* 1949.
PHILOSOPHICAL LIBRARY, INC.
   Einstein, Albert: *Out of My Later Years,* 1950.
   Reichenbach, Hans: *From Copernicus to Einstein,* 1942.
VIKING PRESS
   Sullivan, J. W. N.: *The Limitations of Science,* 1933.

PREFACE

IN 1954 the Anthropological Society of Washington celebrated its 75th Anniversary. In commemoration of this occasion, a coordinated program of lectures was presented to the membership. Since New World archeology is one of the most active fields of anthropological investigations, and one in which many new interpretations have been made recently, it was selected as the subject for the lecture program.

In choosing the speakers for this program, two principal qualifications were kept in mind. We wanted top-notch archeologists who could generalize from their subject matter and derive major interpretative conclusions, and we tried to give preference to those New World areas where the most revolutionary and significant interpretations were being made. For practical reasons, the speakers had to be within reasonable access of Washington, where all the meetings were held.

The program as given included the papers presented here by Drs. Eiseley, Evans, Willey, Ekholm, Spaulding, and Meggers. In addition, one lecture was devoted to a critique of Heyerdahl's *American Indians in the Pacific* with Dr. John M. Corbett evaluating the Peruvian evidence and Dr. Marshall T. Newman appraising the physical anthropology. Since both critiques were principally negative rebuttals of Heyerdahl's thesis and did not make the positive contributions of the other papers, they have not been included in the present volume. Other papers by Drs. Drucker, Reed, and Trager, however, were solicited later to fill in areas and subjects of North America not dealt with by the year's speakers.

In the papers presented here, documentation has been held to a minimum for the purpose of emphasizing the thinking and lending maximum clarity to the interpretations. Each writer is a specialist in the field he covers, has firsthand familiarity with the archeology there, and has full command of the pertinent literature. Bibliographic references therefore are listed only when needed to give the reader access to a fuller presentation of a theory, an illustration of an artifact, or more details on a point of controversy. Thus the goal has been to assemble papers readable to the layman, stimulating to the student, and informative to the anthropologist seeking information on interpretations in areas outside his specialty.

vii

The way the writers handled their interpretations in the New World archeological areas exceeded the expectations of the Society's Program Committee. Excepting Dr. Meggers, none of the writers had previous knowledge of the others' papers; nevertheless, certain basic themes recur in most of them. These themes are pointed out by Dr. Meggers in the concluding paper, and are analyzed for their significance and effect on cultural theory. With essentially the same basic task of presenting reconstructions of cultural development and diffusion in their sections of the Americas, each writer handled his assignment in a different manner. As a result, the papers variously contain much additional information on history of archeological investigations, methods of comparative analysis and interpretation of cultural data, levels of cultural development, effect of environment upon culture, and other problems confronting all anthropologists in the Old as well as the New World.

The 75th Anniversary lecture program was planned by a Program Committee consisting of Drs. Clifford Evans, Betty J. Meggers and Marshall T. Newman. This volume was assembled and edited by Drs. Meggers and Evans. For the Society I wish to express appreciation to the writers for their splendid cooperation, not only in producing the sort of papers we desired, but in presenting their manuscripts in good condition for publication.

MARSHALL T. NEWMAN
President

Anthropological Society of Washington
Smithsonian Institution
Washington 25, D. C.
December, 1954

THE PALEO INDIANS: THEIR SURVIVAL AND DIFFUSION

Loren C. Eiseley

IN TROPICAL RAIN forests scattered around the earth, in island archipelagoes whose tenuous connections with the continents lie sunk beneath the waters of invading seas, a curious array of man's antique relations has lingered into modern times. With few exceptions they are totally arboreal, they are contracted beyond their early Tertiary distributions, and many are relict forms surviving under highly specialized circumstances and in precariously reduced numbers. The forest is their refuge and the warm lands their habitat. Anyone looking at a map of their distribution today might well wonder in what manner their diffusion was achieved. It is a diffusion which hints discreetly of their archaic status and of movements and migrations carried out long ago when the temperature gradient from the poles to the equator was far less steep than it has become during the last million years. They belong to the warm faunas of the earlier part of the Age of Mammals, and it is one of the most curious aspects of primate history, as well as a unique occurrence, that man, one of the descendants of this old-fashioned group of mammals, should have successfully passed northward with a later wave of cold-temperate animals and penetrated the Americas as the most successful and adaptable creature of all time.

Only the student of Holarctic faunas is in a position to recognize the achievement this represents. It is the movement through Holarctica, that Asiatic-American land mass with its swinging draw bridge at Bering Straits and its cold climate filter, which has indirectly affected the entire destiny of life on this planet. That man passed this barrier has more than local significance. Tantalizing though his antiquity in the New World may be, it takes on greatly added significance if we view it in the light of his Asiatic origins. The time of the passing of the bridge, since the bridge constitutes something of an obstacle race, or intelligence test, should tell us a little of the antiquity of man in the Asiatic cradle land, something of his numbers also, and with what sort of fauna he was moving. The antiquity of man in America, therefore, is a problem of world-wide

1

rather than local importance. It constitutes in reality a rough time chart of events elsewhere. For this reason, one cannot say man in America is one hundred thousand or two hundred thousand years old without pausing to consider what this means in the light of our knowledge of the other side of the straits in Asia. Hence, before turning to man's passage southward through the isthmus of Central America, let us glance quickly at his known antiquity in the Old World and what it was that enabled a creature of warm temperate origins to achieve what has been rarely possible to an animal from one of the southern centers of evolution—at least without prolonged physiological adaptation; namely, the passage through the cold filter.

It is a curious fact of biological history that though Darwin once stated his explicit belief in the fact that natural selection can only produce individuals who are slightly more perfect than the rest of the inhabitants of the same region, the truth is that the human brain seems to have exploded upon the world with quite devastating violence and under conditions which seem inadequate on a purely competitive basis to quite account for the more spectacular results. Earlier notions of a long slow incremental increase in cranial capacity, extending over the length of several geological epochs does not, at the present time, seem borne out by the geological and archeological information at our command. A human brain apparently indistinguishable from our own, irrespective of the face that accompanied it, is assured us by William LeGros Clark, in the case of the Swanscombe cranium. A few hundred thousand years earlier in the ill-defined Villafranchian of Africa the last traces of tools fade out and disappear. Over the East African grasslands wander what, for lack of a better term, we may call the animal men, whose cultural status is totally obscure if not actually lacking, and who can only be distinguished as human or pseudo-human by the fact that they stood upright. The remains of the true horse genus Equus have been reported from some, though not all, of these deposits. It is thus evident that they must lie along the Plio-Pleistocene border because Equus is American in origin and its appearance is generally regarded as denoting the beginning Pleistocene. The Australopithecine man-apes, in other words, though quite probably extending into upper Pliocene times cannot certainly be pushed across the Plio-Pleistocene border.

If higher forms of man were in existence at this time, there is no evidence of them either in the shape of bones or humanly flaked artifacts. It would thus appear that whether all the man-apes are on the direct line of human ascent or not, it is impossible, at present, to establish any Pliocene men whose intelligence was in any way superior to theirs. This brings us to a point perhaps less than one million years remote from us, in which

2

the human brain as we know it did not exist, and in which bipedal apes were part of a warm-temperate fauna confined, in all likelihood, to Southern Asia and Africa. Teilhard de Chardin has come out boldly for an African origin of man, but the presence of a possible Australopithecine, *Meganthropus,* in the middle Pleistocene of Java, and earlier fragmentary remains of possibly Australopithecine character in the Nagri formation of India, makes this still a debatable question.

If we plunge boldly into the lower Pliocene and attempt to assess its relationship to intercontinental migration and, indirectly, to the human story, we find a remarkably uniform "faunal sheet," as it has been termed, distributed over Eurasia and North Africa. This fauna, generally spoken of as Pontian "consists . . . of a warm-climate Eurasian fauna that expanded vigorously at this time not only in the subtropics, but also into temperate latitudes . . ." (Simpson, 1947, p. 670). The major aspect of this fauna never reached the American continent. Although our evidence is of a very scanty character, it is legitimate to speculate that the favorable climate conditions which contributed to the rise and differentiation of the Pontian fauna may have promoted the rise and tropical spread of the proto-human man-apes. Antelopes are widespread in this assemblage as are giraffes and hyaenids. There is a suggestive savanna aspect to this world somewhat like that within which we observe the African Australopithecines to be living at a later date. Moreover, the remains regarded by Senyurek and others as hinting at Australopithecine affinities come from the Nagri formation in India which is the Indian time equivalent of the Pontian. These remains consist of the parabolic palate and reduced canines of a creature perhaps ancestral to the South African man-apes.. It is also quite likely that some of the numerous Dryopithecid fragments from the Siwalik hills may be related to this horizon. The point to be emphasized, however, is that the antelopes and other members of this fauna seem in the words of Simpson "visibly attenuated even in still relatively low latitudes in China" (Ibid.). Proto-man, cultureless, naked, or semi-naked is certainly a tropical emergent; the maximum expansion he could have achieved at this stage of his career would have had to be a south temperate Pontian expansion. Nor is it likely he expanded even to the limits of the Pontian northward penetration. In terms of numbers, he was apparently under no excessive population pressure and this means that physiologically he was undergoing no biological selection to withstand extremes of cold. Possible cultural adaptation, it now seems evident, can be ignored as a factor in human diffusion on this time level.

Rather, man may have been largely undergoing severe selection because of the strains and stresses involved in the first adjustment of his body to

3

the upright posture. Profound neurological changes and physical adaptations involving the feet, the position of the vital organs, care of the young, and so forth, must have involved considerable biological wastage and failures of instinct.

The psychiatrist Leonard Sillman, for example, remarked only recently:

"Man, in his emergence, acquired one of the cruelest and most generous endowments ever given to a species of life by a mysterious providence. For thereby a life form arose denuded of the innate reflex instincts which, tried and tested through millions of years of biological experience, constitute each form's most precious inheritance. No other species comes into the world with so few fixed reactions for survival, knows less inherently how to maintain itself. In no other form of life are the instincts so malleable, so changeable in object, so easy to reverse into their opposites" (1953, p. 1).

The penetration of a new ecological niche and subsequent survival within it is often a nip and tuck race with extinction, which must be won before expansion in numbers is possible. To leap from animal to human status was a tremendous, harrowing feat mentally as well as physically. There is no reason to assume that this intensively selective process promoted, in its early stages, a rapid population growth. Instead, we may suspect that man, the animal, was, in a sparse, preparatory sort of way, an insignificant element of the late Pontian fauna. It is my genuine conviction that he will be so established.

We come, then, by way of the land bridge test, to the observation that, accepting the South African ape-men as evidence of some ground ape divergence and expansion during Villafranchian times, man was not physically selected for a cold steppe environment in the lowermost Pleistocene and, further, that such meager cultural beginnings as may have been present were not of a character to promote his passage across the land bridge. His numbers indicate, however, that his major physical adjustment having been achieved he was then on the point of expansion.

Numbers, among simple hunters, cannot be expanded and concentrated in one area, as in the case of the modern urban dweller. There is just so much protoplasm in the shape of food to be passed about. As a consequence, two things must have inevitably occurred: First, a thin but constant spread of the proto-humans over all accessible areas in which survival was possible; in this case the accessible grassland or savanna areas of Africa and Eurasia. Secondly, as the human brain and the growth of language promoted more extended cooperation, there would have been an inevitable shift to the pursuit of bigger and more satisfying pieces of protoplasm in the shape of larger and more dangerous game. Such improvements would even have sustained larger groups in the same territory than

4

could have been fed under the more primitive scavenging and collecting techniques of the animal men. Furthermore, since big animals often move over wide areas to seek food in the shape of new grass, the hunter must often move with them and must inevitably be tempted to follow the trails left by the big beasts. By the middle Pleistocene, we know that palean-thropic man has definitely expanded into all of the temperate areas of the Afro-Eurastic land mass and that, although the bow and spear thrower are not present, he is becoming slowly a more adept hunter apparently capable at times of preying on his own species. The circulation of proto-plasm is beginning to proceed at a faster pace and more of it, from cave bear to fellow man, is passing through the stomach of this new and sinister biped. Moreover, it is conceivable that our warm-temperate to tropical paleanthropic man, in the ebb and flow of two northern glacial advances, has made some slight physiological adjustment to higher latitudes; not to mention his acquisition of fire which, in itself, was one of the first pre-requisites for a passage of the land bridge by a naked tropical animal.

Fire is useful but, for those high latitudes, clothes are of no mean significance either. The interchange of faunas which went on over the Bering Straits land bridge between Asia and North America was, during Pleistocene times, a cold temperate to boreal exchange. Cold steppe bison, woolly mammoth, tundra-loving musk-ox came through. Some of them having a greater climatic and ecological tolerance than the musk-ox were capable of survival in more temperate conditions or of passing southward along suitably grassed highlands.

Now it is an interesting point that the Stipa grasses are regarded by botanists as North American in origin. This genus, in the words of Clem-ents, "has probably played the major role not only in the evolution but also the intercontinental migration of grazing animals" (Goodspeed, 1936, p. 127). The movement of the grasses underwrites and precedes the pas-sage of the Holarctic fauna. It must have been by way of an alley of grass that the passage was achieved and the abundance and advanced evolution of tall, middle, and short American grasses must have been an immediate and fertile stimulus to southward migrants from over the Asiatic bridge during the Pleistocene. It must now be our purpose to examine this alley of grass more closely with an eye to Carbon 14 datings in the New World and with an eye cast upon the human history we have just reviewed.

All of our Carbon 14 datings involved with the earliest traces of man in the New World seem to establish his widespread scattered presence in the interior of the continent in times ranging from about seven thousand to eleven or twelve thousand years ago, and one eight thousand year date has been reported from southern Chile. It would thus appear that man

5

was present and already scattered through both continents very close to the time of the final recession of the Wisconsin glaciation. His cultural remains are frequently associated with the bones of extinct horses, camels, sloths, and elephants—clear and precise evidence that he was relying heavily upon big game for his sustenance—big game that moved in the open, fed upon grasses, and left plainly marked trails.

In every major continent to which the great herbivores have pene- trated, there once ran a series of game trails beaten into the landscape by millions of feet. The trails led to everything that primitive man desired. They ran to water, they ran to salt licks, they found their way across the lowest divides of mountain ranges. In the end, immigrant trails followed some of them and even railroads. Within modern times, they have known the step of the *voyageur* and surveyor. But we have tended to forget that drifting slowly over those trails through endless generations early man, who lacked a nose for water and who did not possess the mysterious com- pass of the migrant birds, nevertheless, found his way through the farthest reaches of the Holarctic land mass. It is by no means impossible that he crossed Bering Straits on such a pathway. Certain it is that he must have marched on many a well-worn southward trail left for him where, ironi- cally, no human foot had ever trod.

In making this observation, it is not necessary to visualize on the part of either men or animals a headlong race to reach the Central Amer- ican isthmus or the regions of the Horn. The men and animals who drifted on those trails in the North were not the ones who arrived in South America. Rather, it was their descendants. What we have to recognize is that men and animals move, and that big animals, and this includes man, tend to travel as population expands,[1] food gets low, or cold winters or dry summers bring unfavorable conditions and hardship. From the game trails of one range there are always trails leading away into other ranges. The horizon is always beckoning and it beckons far more to the grasslander and steppe hunter than to men exploiting a localized forest fauna or a favorable fishing location.

The direction of the great mountain chain ran roughly north to south. It did not bar the way. Actually, the mountains promoted open travel and movement along their flanks. Wedel, for example, has observed in his paper on human ecology in the Central Plains that "Paleo-Indian remains seem to be most plentiful near the mountain front." Their sustenance, he indicates "came primarily from the large mammals." Furthermore, he

---

[1] Childe (1937, p. 66), for example, points out that "the number of upper paleolithic skeletons found in France alone exceeds that of all earlier skeletons put together. Yet the period . . . is not one twentieth of that to which the latter belong."

emphasizes that the "widespread occurrence of such early remains and sites suggests that these foot-hunters were crossing and recrossing the plains on a considerable scale" (1953, p. 504).

The high plains were undoubtedly the first great channel to the south. Moreover, there is every indication that it was a better watered and more fertile channel than today. Traces of dead lakes stretch southward into the barrens of Mexico. Elephants, horse, and bison, which could not subsist in these localities today, have left their bones in mud seeps and lake shore deposits.

Further along in the neck of the isthmus is a wilderness of impenetrable rain forest. We know, however, that in the Pleistocene epoch, elephants, horses, and camels as well as huge ground sloths came through the place where that green barrier stands. It is probable that the road was constricted at this point. Certainly, the bison who ranged as far south as Nicaragua did not penetrate the southern continent, but many others, man among them, did so. It is likely that at this time savanna had not yet been completely replaced by forest. Again, a new world opened out and again along the Andean highlands the way ran southward to the pampas. Man had completed the longest foot journey he was ever to make on the planet.

We have now examined in a brief and summary fashion two sides of a common problem. We have traced the history of man in the Old World up to the middle Pleistocene, and we have seen that this history is surprisingly brief from the geological standpoint. On this side of Bering Straits we see man of the modern species pursuing the last great Pleistocene fauna down the whole length of the world and expanding in the blink of a geological eye over two great continents. On the other side we have noted the slower persistent expansion of the human forerunners though we face a certain paucity of data in establishing, as yet, the precise time of emergence of the first true *Homo sapiens*. It is this item which we need to close the time-gap at Bering Straits.

As a result of Carbon 14 datings secured from the European caves, it is probable that instead of the upper Paleolithic of Europe being assigned a maximum antiquity of, say, fifty thousand years, more conservative dates may now be in order. Movius has intimated that the Skhūl transitionals, or hybrids, may belong in the interstadial between Würm I and II instead of being late third Interglacial. Although we cannot ignore the problem presented by the faceless neurocrania of Swanscombe and Fontechevade, suggestions are made that man, in the modern sense, in his various racial aspects is perhaps no older than the upper Pleistocene. This view is held very tentatively by most workers, however, and is subject to alteration under modern research.

7

Now if we assume, and I think it likely, that man may have passed dry shod or almost so into the New World, the most apt time for this achievement would have been sometime during an interval of ice advance in the Fourth Glaciation. Geologically, this would have meant lowered sea level, thus joining the strait, or almost doing so. It would have encouraged Siberian big game hunters to pass across into comparatively unglaciated Alaska where bison, horse, and elephant appear to have been flourishing.

We need not assume that they passed on southward during the height of the glaciation when the way may have been difficult or blocked. It is, instead, quite conceivable that, like a viscid drop hanging from the spout of a kettle, an Alaskan population group lingered till the way was open and then, multiplying, passed away southward out of the enclosed bridgehead, followed doubtless by later comers. Comparative lack of movement at the strait in later times is not necessarily significant because, as has been noted zoologically, great faunal movements into open lands may take place until an equilibrium is built up, after which very little additional migration will take place even though an accessible bridge still exists.[2] The American Indian, long before white intrusion into the New World, appears to have reached such a balance with Asia. As a consequence, his later history appears more static than could possibly have been the case in late Pleistocene times.

Surveying the remarkable array of local cultures which the spectacle of the two Americas presents, and the great range of environmental conditions which had been mastered, numerous observers were led to postulate periods of many thousand years for the incubation of all these varied developments. The geographer Penck, to use a single example, postulated millenia for man's adaptation to each major climatic zone in the New World.

Now if, in contrast to this approach, we recognize the peculiar and rapid dynamism which has characterized the rise and spread of man, we will escape the fallacy of interpreting man as we now observe him in a score of marginal environments where he has been forced to take no settled ways of life. Much attention has been paid of late to energy in relation to man and the tremendous impact of the neolithic revolution with its accompanying emphasis on agriculture. Childe (1937) has made very vivid the almost endless ramifications of this development and the energy it released in human society.

It is my contention that this revolution was preceded by an earlier

---

[2] For this reason, I see no real clash between my position and that of my colleague Louis Giddings (1952) who is essentially considering a later and basically more static situation. Those interested should also consult J. L. Cotter's (1954) paper. Cotter notes "his tools were portable, often being carried far from their raw material origin. . . ."

economic revolution of almost equal importance[3] but which has been lost in obscurity because it preceded the rise of literate cultures. Moreover, these later cultures, which arose at the time of the collapse, so to speak, of the earlier economy, got only such impoverished glimpses of this earlier way of life that their scholars have professed to see in it man's uttermost infancy of effort. We observe the few peoples still practicing this economy and tend to see, in these feeble tribal units scattered and isolated on the very edges of the world, the miserable conditions under which our fore-fathers existed. This is, I believe, a biased and confused interpretation of the single great revolution that carried a tropical, naked animal of only moderate endurance successfully through the great cold filter and opened to his exploitation all of the major continents. I refer to the simple innova-tion of big game hunting as that economy came to be practiced in upper paleolithic times with elaborate projectile weapons, exquisite flint work, and extended societal cooperation. It is a striking coincidence that with the acquisition of this type of economy, man passes over the world and spills his numbers down the continents in a way he will not do again until the time of the Neolithic Revolution.

It may furthermore be observed that in this economy we have an answer to the theory expressed by some, that man's wide distribution at the end of the Pleistocene is in itself an argument for the great antiquity of *Homo sapiens,* since it implies a very long, slow augmentation of numbers and similar slow expansion over Holarctica. Instead, it would appear that this first food revolution was perhaps almost as explosive as the later economic revolutions, and probably took but little more time to achieve its effects. These effects, not being so directly interpretable in the shape of elaborate city ruins, have been in some degree overlooked.

Two things are seemingly involved in this dramatic and long obscured event: First, the emergence of *Homo sapiens,* who in brain and length of limb seems ideally suited at last for the movement over the world's grass lands; and secondly, the existence of a hunter's paradise almost throughout the earth, great herbivores of immense size and weight, steaks without price if they could be taken, food for whole clans, herds without end, the last great fauna of the closing Pleistocene roving untouched throughout Holarctica. In the words of Professor W. A. Albrecht, the soils specialist,

"Nutritious herbages and dense animal populations dominate in regions of lower rainfalls and moderate temperatures because the less weathered soils of higher fertility make for better nutrition" (1943, p. 222).

---

[3] Childe (1937, p. 65 ff.) hints of the importance of this development in upper paleolithic Europe but does not pursue its Holarctic significance.

As we have seen, men had eaten meat long before this, but it is plain that the thinly strewn animal men by their very paucity of tools must have been collectors, pursuers of insects, chasers of small mammals, cadgers around the kills of the great carnivores. The search for food must have gone on incessantly, and the expenditure of energy compared with intake must have left only a narrow margin of safety.

Indeed this situation is well-nigh caricatured in the extraordinarily brutal facial structure of *Paranthropus crassidens* with its enormous massive muzzle and sagittal crest, as though most of its energies had gone into the production of a magnificent, almost hyaenid, bone-cracking dentition with accompanying musculature. The impression given is that of a proto-human gone all to mouth rather than brain.

Looking back one can say that man has been a fortunate animal or an astute one. The grasslands beckoned to him at a crucial moment in his career before his body had been too firmly set in a brachiating pattern. Thus he attained bipedal progression and freed his hands. Here in the closing Ice Age he seized on the one unlimited source of free energy in the fats and proteins of the supremely successful and swarming grass eaters themselves. He stole their energy for his own, he multiplied at their expense, and he achieved that energy transformation in the quickest manner possible—as a carnivore—the most deadly that had ever walked the planet. It was in this manner that his numbers swept in a few soundless millennia across the earth. Only the great migrations of the Nineteenth Century when industrial Europe poured its millions across the Atlantic are to my mind comparable, though the scale is quite a different one.

He did not need to achieve highly localized adaptations or learn with care and caution and endless experiment the virtues of local plants. To be sure he made some use of these things, but it was all incidental, incidental to eating through the world's wild beef herds like tent caterpillars going through an elm. Then, some ten millennia ago, the great herds failed at last. Why, is still unclear, but certain it is that man contributed to the final disappearance of at least the slowest breeding and hugest bodied. It may be significant that some of these creatures lasted longest in the continents man entered last. At any rate at the close of the Pleistocene, man had passed with what amounts to a single, little varied technology to the ends of the earth. It was big game that had carried him so speedily across the zones, game that supplied his incredible energy to breed, game that had clothed him against the fluctuating vagaries of the Fourth Ice advance.

The passing of so many of the big far-ranging herbivores made the old type of travel difficult, particularly in faunally impoverished areas. The continents were full, measured, that is, by the resources man had then at his command. People would grow more conscious of the land they exploited. The time had come when men sought to hold their place rather than to move, and when accumulating pressures would force men to experiment with what were, until the decimation of the grassland fauna, largely marginal habitats. They would try their hand at working out survival in the low tropical rain forests, or wander from shellfish bed to shellfish bed on sandy and interminable coasts. They would be among those half-wild creatures whom Darwin met in dark, inhospitable waters by the Horn.

Man had run his general course. He had matched wits with all the huge Cenozoic mammals and had emerged triumphant, but over many areas the great herds were gone. They had streamed away at last like the melting glaciers. Man was at grips with poverty again. He would have to huddle and conserve once more, eat insects in dry places, try his teeth on local lizards, poke about with sticks for little things. Still, his mind was busy, he remembered occasional things from lean hunts in the past. The women—patient and observant seed collectors and harvesters—began once more to be heard, while old hunters reminisced wistfully about the last mammoth.

The next revolution, the attack on the plants, would not move so rapidly. Some tribes on the world's margins would never enjoy it. They would have to take what they could of the things that remained, or, as many were later to do, fall into symbiotic relationships with food growers. It may be that many starved even though the hunters had always spread fast but thinly. Now would come the long growth of the local cultures, the slow rise of the next great food revolution gotten out of patience rather than violence. The concentration of population in agricultural areas would begin. The world's vacuums were filled and the trails of mammoth would fade away under the grass, just as, at Bering Straits, the water now lapped over that wonderful pathway that had brought man into the last great Eden of the world.

PREHISTORIC CULTURAL DEVELOPMENT IN THE EASTERN UNITED STATES

Albert C. Spaulding

THE PROBLEM of presenting a meaningful and compact description of the general course of cultural events in the prehistoric United States is a troublesome one. The essential difficulty lies in the fact that the evidence is by no means complete and unequivocal, so that the describer seems to be faced by the equally undesirable alternatives of sketching a neat outline of dubious accuracy or of overwhelming the reader with a mass of factual but incoherent detail. Obviously, an attempt must be made to convey some sense of the character of the empirical data, the nature of the interpreta-tive principles thought to be relevant, and the results obtained by applica-tion of the principles to the data, and at the same time to avoid the diffi-culties inherent in these alternatives. With this end in view, I shall try to classify the assemblages of tools and other remnants of aboriginal com-munities which constitute the "givens" of archeology with respect to cul-ture type, time, and geographical position, and then to combine these classifications in order to show significant relationships and perhaps to gain some insight into the processes and causes that operated in the prehis-toric past.

An essential step in this procedure is the classification of the assem-blages (often called components in archeological literature) with respect to their resemblance to each other. Resemblance here means actual physical similarity of tools, utensils, remains of houses, and so on. It means in addi-tion quantitative similarity, a concept which includes not only the form and other physical properties of the artifacts but also the relative popularity of artifact types in the components being compared. I will refer to the groups of components resulting from this sort of classification by the con-veniently vague term "culture type," which means a group of components distinguishable by the common possession of a group of traits. The statisti-cally minded can conceive of a culture type as a group of components exhibiting a significant cluster of traits. Since nothing has been said as to the nature of the traits used in investigating the clustering, it is apparent

12

that quite different orders of grouping can fall within the broad category of a culture type; the group of components included in a single culture type in one system of classification may resemble each other very closely indeed, perhaps down to such details as the number and placement of notches on arrow points, while in another system broad similarities such as the cultivation of maize may be the criteria for inclusion. The nature of the attributes selected will depend upon the nature of the problem which the investigator is trying to solve with the aid of his typological investigations.

A second necessary step is classification of components with respect to time, one of the fundamental dimensions of culture change. Under ideal circumstances, we would simply arrange the components in their proper rank as shown by their calendar dates and then define chronological periods in terms of important cultural innovations. Unfortunately, circumstances are far from ideal, and we are forced to adopt a less satisfactory approach in most cases. The basic methods of investigating the time relationship of any two components consist of such techniques as discovery of relative age by direct superposition or a demonstrable relationship of both components to some third event, or of estimating absolute age of both by some year count or rate-quantity method. In the case of a number of components exhibiting varying degrees of likeness, another kind of chronological ordering can be made on the assumption that the components which resemble each other most closely culturally are also closest together in time. This sort of ordering is known as "seriation." The year count and rate-quantity methods are theoretically of the greatest importance; a determination of absolute age (in terms of years ago) not only gives the temporal order of events but also reveals the speed with which the events took place. For the eastern United States, there is only one important method of measuring absolute time, the rate-quantity radiocarbon test, although the year count tree ring technique seems to have great promise in some specialized local situations. Certain inherent limitations of both methods indicate that they will never entirely supplant seriation and superposition as tools for interpretation.

The third major criterion of component classification is geographical space. Here the fundamental attribute of geographical position is not inferred or reconstructed but rather is given as a part of our empirical data. However, the manner in which the individual geographical positions of the components should be grouped is not at all clear at first blush. This discussion is already committed by title to one sort of grouping, the cultures of the eastern United States, and I hope to show that this choice of geographical unit is not altogether an arbitrary one. Later in the paper

I will bring up the question of the sort of geographical groupings exhibited by the components of various culture types and the inferences which can be drawn from such groupings.

If we view the ultimate task of archeology as the development of the ability to explain the similarity or lack of similarity of any two components, the significance of these three kinds of classifications is easy to state. All can be related to the proposition that culture change is systematic rather than capricious and to the auxiliary proposition that an important basis for the systematic behavior of culture is its continuous transmission through the agency of person to person contact. The observed degree of similarity between the two components sets the problem to be solved, and time and geographical position are two discrete systems, each of which offers an independent measure of closeness. We would expect that two components closely associated in geographical space and time would resemble each other closely in culture type; conversely, we would expect that two components not resembling each other closely would be well separated in time or in geographical position or in both. All of this reasoning does not imply that the relationships are strictly proportional, however; there is abundant evidence to show that culture can and characteristically does change through time and space at varying rates, thereby saving archeology from the fate of being a simple exercise in multiplication and division. A major part of the problem of the archeology of the eastern United States is precisely this situation—explanation of shifts in culture type in a comparatively small region when there is either no evidence of substantial time difference or there is evidence that no great amount of time separates the differing culture types.

Under these circumstances, it will be necessary to invoke other explanatory principles. One of these principles is concerned with geography on an ecological basis, or, more broadly, in terms of cultural opportunities and restrictions offered by the animals, plants, climate, and so on of differing natural regions. Another is a sort of residual principle, the category of explanations often called "historical," which are essentially special accounts of the particular conditions involved in some event or set of events. A distressing feature of historical explanations is their perverse tendency to be nearly as complicated as the conditions they purport to explain, but I think all archeologists will agree that the happy day when we can dispense with such homely crutches in favor of unexceptionable generalizations lies a very great distance in the future. An example of this sort of explanation which appears later in this discussion is the proposition that agriculture appeared in the eastern United States as a result of the immigration of a group already having agriculture. Although this is a

14

genuine explanation from our circumscribed geographical outlook, it contributes nothing positive toward solving the broader problem of the origin of American agriculture.

With this theoretical background in mind, I will turn to the descriptive section of the discussion, a characterization of selected culture types of the area. No attempt will be made to cover thoroughly every subarea and every detail of each culture type. Instead, an effort will be made to choose the features and examples of each culture type which will bring into sharp focus the fundamental problems of the area. Four groupings of components appear to be adequate for this purpose, omitting the problem of the Paleo-Indian because it has already been discussed in this series. These culture types are conventionally known as the Archaic Culture, the Adena Culture, the Hopewell Culture, and the Middle Mississippi Culture.

THE ARCHAIC CULTURE

The Archaic Culture type is a rather shaky classificatory union of a large number of small components scattered over practically the entire area under consideration. Indeed, the reported presence of Archaic sites in any particular region seems to be pretty much a function of the intensity of archeological field work. The major unifying feature of the Archaic components on the positive side is the small size of the sites (this statement will be qualified later) and the presence of large flint projectile points, although this is not meant to imply that small sites and large projectile points are absent from other culture types. It is much easier to describe the Archaic sites in terms of what is absent from them; they do not show pottery, smoking pipes, mounds and other earth construction, or evidence of substantial buildings, and these absences are good evidence for their generally early time position. It has been inferred from the negative evidence that the Archaic peoples gained their subsistence through hunting, fishing, and gathering rather than agriculture. Dart throwers were certainly used to hurl projectiles (actual specimens have been found), and the prevailingly large flint projectile points suggest that the bow and arrow were entirely unknown.

It is clear from the information at hand that significant cultural subgroupings existed at the Archaic level. There were western variants, for example the non-pottery sites discovered by the Smithsonian River Basin Surveys in recent years. Farther to the east, complexes which come to mind are the distinctive and well-known shell heap sites of the Savannah, Tennessee, and Green Rivers; a variety of coastal sites from Maine to Florida (often marked by extensive shell heaps); an aberrant non-pottery culture in the lower Mississippi Valley best known from the sites of Jaketown in Mississippi and Poverty Point in Louisiana; and two cultural entities in New York and New England, the Lamoka Culture and another sometimes called the Laurentian Culture. The differences observed between these groupings are in large part to be explained on geographical grounds to judge by the quite well-defined regions into which the component sites cluster. It is probably fair to say that much of the observed variation can be attributed to regional developments from a common and widespread Paleo-Indian base. But certain of the differences are of such nature as to suggest that time differences within the period of Archaic Culture domination and derivation from distinctive cultural backgrounds are also to be considered.

A brief comparison of four of the Archaic sub-units mentioned above will illustrate the problem. The first of these is the Indian Knoll Culture of the Green River in Kentucky, a representative of the southeastern river-shell-heap type of culture. The Indian Knoll people lived on the river banks in favored spots where mussels were abundant. They were deer hunters, fishermen, and gatherers of the local flora and river mussels. Although an Indian Knoll community was at any one time undoubtedly a small village (probably no more than a hundred or so persons), continual occupation for a very long period resulted in impressive refuse deposits composed primarily of tons of mussel shells, abundant deer and other animal bones, and other debris. The refuse mounds are almost literally riddled with burial pits, and the grave goods found in them demonstrate that some leisure was available for the production of beautifully finished polished stone dart thrower weights, bone and antler dart throwers, nicely decorated bone pins, stone and shell beads, and other luxury goods. The presence of conch shells from Florida waters and copper from the Lake Superior region clearly shows that the extensive trade routes of later periods had their inception here. Heavy woodworking was accomplished with fully grooved stone axes, and a variety of chipped flint scrapers and knives served for lighter tasks. Large flint projectile points are, of course, commonly found, and numerous stone pestles suggest preparation of vegetable food. The relatively early time position of the Indian Knoll Culture type is plain because, like other Archaic complexes, it lacks a number of traits universally present in the area in protohistoric and early historic times. This inferential dating is amply confirmed by eight radiocarbon dates ranging from about 5000 B.C. to about 2000 B.C.

At approximately the same time, on the basis of radiocarbon dating, a second Archaic Culture type existed in western New York. It is best

16

known from a site at Lamoka Lake and is usually called the Lamoka Culture. Although the subsistence pattern of the Lamoka people must have
been much like that reported from Indian Knoll and many similarities in
artifact types can be detected, there are also significant differences. Work
in marine shells is virtually absent at Lamoka, and the grooved axe of
Indian Knoll does not occur at all, its place as a heavy woodworking tool
being taken by crude flaked stone choppers and several kinds of polished
stone adzes. There are enough differences in the bone and antler tools to
characterize them as overlapping but distinctive assemblages. It can hardly
be argued that such differences in detail were a direct response to sharply
distinct environmental circumstances—Kentucky is not so different from
New York as all that and there is no particular reason to think that the
two regions were less like each other a few thousand years ago. Moreover, the actual distance between the cultures was not great, and there is
no formidable geographical barrier intervening. Under these circumstances,
the explanation which seems most likely is that Lamoka and Indian Knoll
were peripheral representatives of culture types which did develop in relative isolation under distinctly different ecological circumstances. The main
ties of Indian Knoll are clearly to the southeast, where numerous sites of
similar character are found. On the other hand, the Lamoka Culture has
certain northern overtones. Thus the beveled adze is found in greatest
quantity along the north shores of Lake Erie and Lake Ontario, and a
preference for the adze as a woodworking tool is a strong and ancient boreal
tradition from Scandinavia to Labrador. The Lamoka beaver tooth knives
point in the same direction. However, Lamoka can scarcely be thought of
as a transplanted boreal culture owing to the absence of certain common-
place northern artifact types, especially barbed bone points. It would seem
to be basically a variant of the eastern United States Archaic Culture type
which was influenced to a certain extent by the alien culture of the spruce-
fir forests to the north.

A third subtype which falls within the very broad definition of Archaic
is the poorly defined Laurentian Culture, a term which I will use to include
a number of manifestations scattered from Wisconsin to New England.
Although we are handicapped by a bad sampling situation, some evidence
of local specialization, and probably time difference, it is possible to describe
the Laurentian Culture as producing a variety of chipped stone forms,
barbed bone points, winged bannerstones, ground slate and copper projectile
points, and ground stone and copper adzes and gouges. Stratigraphic evidence indicates that the Laurentian succeeds the Lamoka Culture in New
York, and it apparently persisted for a time after the introduction of pottery. From our standpoint, the important feature of the Laurentian is that

17

it cannot be derived satisfactorily from the preceding cultures. It represents a new complex of elements associated with a new physical type in the northeastern part of our area. The gouges, ground slate points, and other elements point to a northern origin, and an actual movement of people from the Canadian forest seems to be the most likely explanation. The ultimate origin of the Laurentian complex need not concern us here, but it is surely in some sense a representative of the north European-Siberian-North American cultural tradition of the boreal forest zone, and its appearance in the northeastern fringe of our area is a reflection of the proximity of that fringe to the northern forests. Indeed, certain parts of the area of Laurentian occupancy such as the Upper Peninsula of Michigan can be considered essentially of boreal forest type from the standpoint of ecology.

A final special subtype of the Archaic to be discussed is the Poverty Point complex of Louisiana and Mississippi. It is included with the Archaic Cultures because of its lack of pottery vessels, but in many respects it is a strange bedfellow. The culture is not known in every detail, but outstanding features of Poverty Point sites include great quantities of more or less crudely modeled clay objects of unknown function. Fragments of stone vessels are also a characteristic feature. It is thought that the vessels were imported from the southern Appalachian region, the nearest available source of the soapstone and closely related minerals used for their manufacture. A still more surprising feature is the recent discovery of large numbers of small, ribbon-like blades of flint at several sites; their association with the other Poverty Point materials is not certain but seems highly probable. The most striking feature of all, however, is the presence of earthworks. At the Poverty Point site itself these include a tremendous octagonal figure composed of six concentric banks of earth, the whole being some three-quarters of a mile in diameter, and a mound 70 feet high situated on the west side of the octagon. The amorphous clay objects, flint work, and earth construction are quite unlike anything reported from other Archaic Cultures, and some sort of special explanation is in order. Geographical isolation may be involved in part, but the lower Mississippi Valley is not exactly remote from the Tennessee-Alabama-Georgia area with its more orthodox cultures, and the soapstone is good evidence of actual contact between the two areas. A second explanation is isolation in time from the better known Archaic Cultures, and one radiocarbon date of 400 B.C. supports this line of reasoning. The radiocarbon date produces difficulties almost as formidable as those it is supposed to solve because by this time there were well-established agricutural and pottery making groups in the Illinois-Ohio area. But, if the date is reasonably close, we can derive the earthworks and perhaps the ribbon flakes from the Hopewell Culture as

18

Ford has suggested. The Hopewell Culture (to be discussed below) was a pottery making, agricultural complex, and I am at a loss to explain why the Poverty Point people failed to make pottery of Hopewell type if such a connection existed. A third explanation is that the Poverty Point Culture as described here did not exist at all—that we have assembled a group of incongruous elements on the basis of accidental geographical association. On this view, the clay objects and stone sherds would already have been archeological specimens when the earth embankments and the mound were built. In short, we will leave Poverty Point as an enigma.

Our résumé of the Archaic has discussed four differing culture types. The Indian Knoll type was presented as a characteristic example of a native culture developed in the southeast from a Paleo-Indian base over a period of several thousand years, and it was indicated that related although not identical cultures of similar origin could be found in most parts of the eastern United States. The Lamoka Culture was thought to be fundamentally of the same origin but visibly influenced by an alien tradition at home in the subarctic zone. The Laurentian Culture was said to be derived from the subarctic zone, and the mode of introduction seems to have been outright invasion into the boreal fringe of our area. The Poverty Point Culture was presented as an anomaly which cannot be explained with any degree of satisfaction from the evidence at hand.

THE ADENA CULTURE

We now leave the simple hunters and gatherers for the second of our major culture types, the entity commonly known as the Adena Culture. The Adena Culture is a well-defined type with a restricted geographical range in the southern part of Ohio, southeastern Indiana, northern Kentucky, northwestern West Virginia, and southwestern Pennsylvania. Within this area, and especially in Ohio, there are numerous sites marked by more or less conical burial mounds and sometimes circular or other types of earth bank enclosures. Most of the information about the culture is derived from excavation of the burial mounds and the scanty village site refuse found in the vicinity of the mounds. The mounds and their associated material reveal a culture which is of quite a different order from that of the Archaic people, although the absence of adequate data on village refuse is a serious deficiency in our knowledge of Adena.

On the basis of the sheer size of the mounds (one of them is about 70 feet high) and the complexity of the mortuary practices associated with them, we can safely infer a complex social organization and an efficient

19

economic base. It would appear that on occasion the body of an important dignitary would be placed in a log tomb in a house floor together with artifacts and other bodies, perhaps those of retainers slain for the purpose, and that the tomb would then be covered temporarily. After a suitable interval, the bones would be painted and a small earth mound erected over the tomb. The next step consisted of burning the house containing the tomb and its primary mound, and finally the main mound was constructed over the remains of the burned house, the primary mound, and the tomb. In some cases, additional tombs were placed in the final mound at various stages in its construction. Simple cremation in the village areas seems to have been the prevailing custom for ordinary folk.

Other Adena traits clearly indicate a substantial way of life. Houses were circular with sturdy outward slanting supporting posts; they ranged from about 20 to nearly 70 feet in diameter. There are in addition some circles of post molds about 100 feet in diameter. If the latter were completely roofed, one house would have been capable of sheltering a sizable village. Even the smaller circles indicate houses of very respectable dimensions and capacities. Pottery vessels of simple forms, some having four-footed bases; tubular stone pipes; stone, copper, shell, and mica ornaments; stone celts; textiles; and other artifacts have been found. A human effigy tubular pipe from an Ohio mound shows a man clad in a decorated breech cloth with a bustle-like appendage and wearing circular ear plugs. I think that most archeologists infer that the Adena people cultivated corn, tobacco, gourds, and presumably other plants, although direct evidence is scanty or lacking. Finally, the Adena people were physically quite distinct from the Indian Knoll people of the same general area, and they accentuated this distinctiveness by the practice of head deformation.

If it is true that the Adena culture represents the first appearance of this general cultural complex in the area, and the weight of evidence seems to indicate that it is true, then the question of Adena-Archaic relationships is critical. We should first point out that corn as a cultivated crop is on botanical grounds almost certainly of Middle or South American origin and hence must be an imported trait. It seems equally clear that a reasonably efficient corn agriculture must underlie such an elaborate cultural development, and we are forced to postulate some sort of direct or indirect connection with Middle or South America. That this connection did not take place through the southwestern United States is suggested by the fact that the corn of the closely related and nearly contemporaneous Hopewell Culture is a Guatemalan type not normally found in the early agricultural horizons of the Southwest. It would appear then that northeastern Mexico is the most likely source. An alternative route through the

Antillean islands is said to be most unlikely by specialists in that area. But it is not absolutely certain that Adena is the first corn growing culture of the area on the evidence of radiocarbon dating. One radiocarbon date for a Kentucky Adena site is about 700 B.C., a second for the same site is 220 B.C., but another Kentucky mound yielded a date of A.D. 780 and an Ohio mound dated at A.D. 440. This time range begins a little earlier but for the most part overlaps that of the Hopewell Culture, making it impossible to decide on this evidence alone whether or not the Adena people were the first agriculturalists of eastern United States. Even if we accept the chronological priority of Adena, a view which was standard before radiocarbon dating, we are still in an area of sharp disagreement about the manner in which it originated.

One point of view is that the Adena complex in essentially complete form was brought by a rapid migration from northeastern Mexico to the Ohio valley, thus accounting for the simultaneous appearance of a new physical type and a radically different cultural orientation. Unfortunately, no one has as yet discovered an unmistakable ancestor in the proper part of Mexico. It is not impossible that an appropriate predecessor will be dis' covered in the future, however, and such traits as ear spools, large round houses, celts rather than grooved axes, perhaps burial mounds, burial in house floor, and so on, do have a faintly Middle or even South American flavor. Opponents of this view suggest a bare minimum of Mexican influ' ence—a diffusion of corn and a few other plants without actual migration of people—followed by a local development of burial practices and other elaborate features. Apparent continuities with the local Archaic, for example in chipped stone tools and use of shell and copper, are emphasized, and the new physical type is explained by evolution in place or by a population increment from the north as exemplified by the Laurentian situation. I think that there is not sufficient evidence at hand to attempt any final adjudication of these opposing theories, although I regard the migration theory as less cumbersome. The problem is an extremely impor' tant one because it deals with a fundamental cultural reorientation involving the establishment of a set of basic practices which persisted until the obliteration of Indian culture in the eastern United States.

THE HOPEWELL CULTURE

The Hopewell Culture represents a third distinctive culture type, but its distinctiveness with relation to Adena is a matter of detail rather than of basic subsistence and ceremonial patterns. The geographical distribution

21

and character of Hopewell sites suggest two primary areas of concentration, southern Ohio and the valleys of the Illinois and Mississippi Rivers in Illinois. Other centers with clear Hopewell affinities are found in Louisiana, the Florida coast, the Kansas City area, and in various other localities scattered from New York to Oklahoma. In its most highly developed form, which occurs in southern Ohio, the Hopewell culture produced some exceedingly impressive remains. Very large burial mounds, hilltop enclosures, and literally miles of earthworks arranged in geometrical enclosures and parallel walls are found at Ohio sites and offer the clearest possible evidence of effective group labor. Scarcely less impressive are quantities of fine art products deposited in the burial mounds. Raw materials for these products were imported from such remote sources as the Appa-lachian region of Virginia and North Carolina, the Rocky Mountains, the Lake Superior region, and the Florida coast. The art products and mounds are expressions of an elaborate mortuary cult, and the peculiar geometric shapes of the earthbank enclosures strongly suggest ceremonial functions. Information on ordinary Hopewell village sites is quite scanty, but it can be said that they were comparatively humble with little evidence of impressive permanent buildings or the fine art goods associated with the burial mounds. Subsistence was obtained by gardening (actual examples of corn have been found) and by hunting and gathering wild products. The bow and arrow seem to have been unknown, the dart thrower being the device used to hurl projectiles as was the case with Archaic and Adena Cultures. In general, there is little evidence of notable differences between Adena and Hopewell in basic subsistence techniques. The greater brilliance and geographical extent of the Hopewell Culture accordingly cannot be attributed to any markedly superior economic techniques; it appears rather to be the result of more effective social organization along the general lines introduced by the Adena people.

But Hopewell Culture cannot be considered simply an intensification or elaboration of the Adena pattern. We can logically postulate an Adena source for the basic agriculture and many of the ceremonial practices, especially the earthbank enclosures and burial mounds. It is perhaps justi-fiable to speculate about possible Adena prototypes for such Middle Amer-ican-like Hopewell traits as copper earspools, negative painted cloth, and panpipes. There are, however, other Hopewell traits which point to a direct connection with the Archaic people rather than to the Adena Culture. Examples of such traits are the presence in Hopewell of the grooved stone axe, stone plummets, and cut animal jaws. In this connection, it is important to note that the Hopewell physical type is predominantly that of the Archaic people, although some genetic influence from the Adena people is evident.

A third group of Hopewell elements does not look like either the Middle Western Archaic or like Adena, but seems rather to have a northern stamp; here one can include ribbon-like flint flakes used as knives, conoidal bottomed pottery finished with a cord-wrapped paddle and decorated by impressions of a cord-wrapped stick or a toothed tool, bilaterally symmetrical decoration reminiscent of northern art in birchbark, and skin moccasins (shown on clay figurines). A final group of culture elements was surely invented by the Hopewell people themselves. An excellent example is the characteristic platform smoking pipe.

When we add to these factors the radiocarbon dates for Hopewell (beginning slightly later but having roughly the same range as those of Adena), the following interpretation is suggested:

1. Following the introduction of the Adena Culture, it dominated its restricted area and strongly influenced an Archaic population to the west, particularly in Illinois. This population had already received influence from the north, just as did the Archaic people of New York.

2. Archaic, Adena, and northern influences fused into a vigorous Hopewell Culture which expanded to the east and took over the Adena area in Ohio but not in northern Kentucky, where the Adena people were able to maintain their cultural and physical identity for a considerable period.

3. Concurrently, Hopewell ideas and to some extent Hopewell people expanded widely over the eastern United States. It seems likely that in many areas the Hopewell rather than the Adena people were responsible for the introduction of burial mounds and agriculture, and that many simple mound-building, pottery-making groups now considered to be pre-Hopewell were actually contemporaneous with Hopewell.

4. There followed a period of decline marked by abandonment of the great Ohio and Illinois ceremonial centers and development of a number of local traditions which carry on certain of the Hopewell ideas in an impoverished form.

The reader is warned that this reconstruction is based upon something less than universally accepted evidence; indeed, it is no more than a point of view from which to reappraise existing evidence and to seek new data. It is impossible to predict whether or not future work will confirm or deny the general scheme, but it does seem to account best for the material at hand.

There does not appear to be any simple explanation for the fading out of Hopewell Culture. Certainly, there is no clear evidence of military conquest by incoming peoples or the advent of any sweeping economic

23

changes. Whatever the reason, or reasons, for the decline may have been, it does seem to be true that in most (or perhaps all) of the areas of highly developed Hopewell Culture an interlude of comparatively simple cultures separates the Hopewell peak from the next great culture type, the Middle Mississippi.

THE MIDDLE MISSISSIPPI CULTURE

In the strictest sense, the Middle Mississippi Culture type is repre-sented by a limited number of great sites situated roughly in an east-west belt from north central Georgia through northern Alabama and Mississippi to western Tennessee and Kentucky, southern Illinois, and southeastern Missouri. In addition to these great centers, Middle Mississippi influences radiated far and wide to modify outlying groups which had strong cultural roots in the preceding period. Outstanding elements in the new cultural configuration are (1) tremendous ceremonial centers having a plaza arrange-ment of pyramidal temple mounds and sometimes a ditched and palisaded fortification; (2) large village sites (not always directly associated with mound groups) with accompanying cemeteries; (3) a new pottery com-plex in which the clay was mixed with crushed burned shell, many new vessel forms were made, and handles, modeled decoration, and painting were emphasized; (4) a number of new art concepts executed in clay, carved stone, sheet copper, engraved shell, and other media; and (5) various other new types of artifacts, of which an example is a small triangular arrow point of flint.

Dating of Middle Mississippi Culture on the more recent end of the scale offers no difficulty; the culture was flourishing when the De Soto party made its way across the southeast in the mid-sixteenth century. The problem of how far back in time it extends is not so easy. Existing radio-carbon dates for Middle Mississippi sites are capricious and internally incon-sistent, but it seems safe to estimate that the earlier sites were in existence by about A.D. 1000. There is evidence of cultural development within the Middle Mississippi tradition in the form of changing pottery styles and the addition of new motifs in ceremonial art, but cultures that are plainly transitional between Hopewell and Middle Mississippi are not known.

This absence of developmental stages suggests the importation of ideas to the eastern United States, and the pyramidal mounds and the art forms again point to Mexico as the source. Portrayals of winged snakes, dancing men with bird attributes and speech scrolls issuing from their mouths, human skulls and long bones, and other items have a definite Middle

24

American appearance, although no object of actual Mexican origin has been reported. But the new culture is not plainly associated with a new physical type, there is no evidence of linguistic connection with Mexico, and many Middle Mississippi traits have their origin in the Hopewell or earlier periods in the United States. It looks very much as if a group of Mexican religious ideas and perhaps forms of social organization was added to, and assimilated by, the native post-Hopewell Culture. The small arrow points probably signify the replacement of the older dart thrower by the bow and arrow as the major weapon for warfare and hunting, but it is not known whether or not new crops or important new varieties of old crops appeared. In any case, the very large size of the ceremonial centers and villages testifies to a productive economic system, an effective social organization, and a preoccupation with religious activities.

The mechanism by which such a cultural change could be effected can only be guessed at. Some sort of contact with Mexico, again probably northeastern Mexico on geographical grounds, is indicated, and the contact must have been of such nature as to permit the dissemination of ideas without extensive movement of material objects or people. Perhaps the rich ceremonialism and generally impressive level of Mexican cultures proved irresistible to visitors from Missouri or Arkansas, who returned to their homeland as missionaries with a vivid impression of Mexican religious ideas and paraphernalia. Certainly, the Pueblo area of New Mexico and Arizona cannot be the source of the Mexican influence since Middle Mississippi was in some respects much closer to Mexican practices than were the Pueblo peoples. For example, pyramidal mounds are entirely unknown in the Pueblo country at any period.

CONCLUSION

Our description of the culture history of the eastern United States has been a highly selective one which emphasized turning points and climaxes. In every case, a great deal of space could have been employed in describing cultural manifestations which did not represent the most intensive expressions of the successive culture types. By ignoring these peripheral cultures and by nearly ignoring continuities between the culture types which were discussed, I have obscured a major feature of the area, the fact that no complete break in cultural tradition occurred from the Archaic period to the European conquest. This point of view contrasts sharply with a great deal of earlier theorizing which characteristically postulated migrations to account for even minor cultural changes, and it is supported both by the

25

archeological evidence of cultural continuity and by the evidence of systematic distribution of biological characteristics presented by Newman. In
only one case have we resorted to migration to explain a significant new
culture type, that of the Adena people and the extremely important introduction of agriculture from Middle America, and even this is doubted by
many archeologists.

Thus the situation in the main is one of a comparatively stable Paleo-
Indian population from the Plains to the Atlantic coast. By the Archaic
period, and probably even in Paleo-Indian times, regional culture types had
developed in response to the particular opportunities and demands of the
several ecologically differing regions. The subsequent picture is one of the
introduction of new trait complexes which were promptly modified to con-
form to the already existing regional traditions, so that at any given time
clearly delineated and geographically compact culture types existed. Indeed,
it seems fair to say that the historic culture areas maintained their identity
through widespread major shifts in culture type. At the same time, the
eastern United States as a whole has been a distinguishable cultural unit
throughout our long chronological period. At no time has there been substantial identity with the Pueblo area, although a few traits may have been
exchanged between the two areas. The cultures of the boreal forest zone
may have transmitted a few Asiatic traits to the Middle West and Northeast, but their influence can hardly be regarded as marked except on the
actual borders in the Great Lakes area and the extreme northeast. Middle
American influence was certainly profound, since we must credit this area
with the origin of agriculture and a number of other ideas, but in no case
did any invading Mexican or Antillean peoples eliminate native populations and native ways of doing things. The story is rather one of an essentially unitary development fertilized but never obliterated by alien traditions.

A BIBLIOGRAPHIC NOTE

The published sources on the archeology of the eastern United States
are very numerous, and I have made no attempt to buttress my discussion
with footnote references to original statements of facts or ideas. Any validity that the interpretation presented may have is the result of the work of
a great many people over a considerable period of time; errors are, of
course, solely my responsibility. Two ideas of other authors which were
specifically mentioned are described in "Additional Notes on the Poverty
Point Site in Northern Louisiana," by James A. Ford (*American Anti-*

quity, Volume XIX, pp. 282-284, 1954) and in Marshall T. Newman's "The Application of Ecological Rules to the Racial Anthropology of the Aboriginal New World," (*American Anthropologist*, Volume 55, pp. 311-327, 1953). The most recent general treatment of the area is *Archeology of Eastern United States*, edited by James B. Griffin (Chicago, 1952). For still more recent information, the best approach is a survey of *American Antiquity*, the journal of the Society for American Archaeology.

THE INTERRELATED RISE OF THE NATIVE CULTURES OF MIDDLE AND SOUTH AMERICA

Gordon R. Willey

INTRODUCTION

The peaks of native American civilization were attained in the Middle American regions of Mexico and Guatemala and in Peru[1] in the two millennia preceding the Spanish conquests of the 16th century. These two summits of New World cultural achievement are widely separated from each other by the intervening areas of lower Central America, Colombia, and Ecuador. What is the significance of this geographical separation? To what degree does it reflect a cleavage in the common histories of Peruvian and American cultures? To what extent may the similarities that exist be derived from historical interconnections? Or may these similarities be attributed to factors of independent growth? These questions have long been a matter of interest and speculation.

The considerable literature centering upon these themes is too much to summarize within the scope of this paper; however, certain writings seem particularly important because they show the development of a very definite body of theory concerned with this problem. As early as 1917, H. J. Spinden conceived of a fundamental underlying cultural substratum for all New World high cultures, which he called "Archaic." This was a sort of American "neolithic" diffusion representing the spread of a seden-tary-agricultural way of life from Middle America to the north and to the south. In spite of specific defects, this hypothesis in its broader aspects is still an operational theory in American archeology. A. L. Kroeber (1930) developed a similar line of reasoning when he visualized the Mexican and Peruvian culture climaxes as rising from the same historically interrelated

---

[1] For the purposes of this paper, these areas are defined as the southern one-half to one-third of Mexico, all of Guatemala and British Honduras, parts of Salvador, Honduras, and perhaps Nicaragua and Costa Rica, or the "Mesoamerican" area as defined by Kirchoff (1943), the Peruvian coast and highlands and the adjacent Bolivian altiplano, or essentially the area defined by Bennett (1946) as the "Central Andes."

platform of technology and basic cultural content. The same food plants, the same kinds of ceramic, textile, metallurgical, and architectural achievements appeared to him as indisputable linkages. He saw Middle America and Peru as alike in that both drew upon this common background to give "finer form" or "more intensive organization or expression" (op. cit., p. 21) to the materials of their mutual American heritage.

In the two decades since Kroeber's synthesis, archeological research in both the Andean and Middle American areas has moved ahead rapidly, particularly with regard to the definition of culture sequences and the integration of these into relative chronologies of area-wide scope (Kroeber, 1948b). W. D. Strong (1943) has shown how Middle-to-South American comparisons take on sharpness of definition when these comparisons can be made with proper regard for their chronological order. Julian H. Steward (1949b) has utilized the same sequence data described by Strong for correlating the two areas period for period from a different point of view. Steward's interest has been functional development. He tends to take diffusion between the two Americas for granted and concentrates on the question: What does diffusion amount to as an explanation of culture growth and process? Rather than comparing specific content, Steward turns to overall cultural configurations in the major periods within each area. It is here that he notes a series of strong similarities in the rise and development of socio-political, religious, and military institutions.

In the present discussion, I am interested in reviewing the case for DIFFUSION between the centers of American high culture but I do not mean to minimize developmental analyses. Diffusion and independent invention are, after all, polar abstractions concerning complex human events and the two processes work in concert. Nevertheless, the tracing out of diffusion remains a respectable anthropological problem. It is not the whole story but it is an important part of the story. Let us turn, then, to the evidence for culture contact between Middle and South America and observe the patterning of this evidence in space and in time.

In doing so, it might be well to pause to review the nature of the evidence we are to consider. In a brief paper, it is impossible to cover all of the data that have been brought forward by many scholars on this complex subject of inter-American cultural connections. In this treatment, some categories of evidence such as linguistic and physical anthropometric details will be ignored. From ethnographical records, there are a number of traits which almost certainly have a common history and which link Middle and South America. The arrow sacrifice of captives is an example often cited. The rubber ball game, which is known in lowland South America and throughout Middle America, is another. There is little doubt but what these features or ideas have been transmitted intercontinentally but it is extremely difficult, if not impossible, to pin down their occurrences in the contexts of archeological sequences. Either no traces are left in the archeological records or the traits are of such a nature that they might well be passed from one region to another without leaving any clues that could be appraised chronologically from archeological evidence. For the present study, then, we are restricting the evidence to a certain limited number of traits or elements which are verifiable by archeological means and which also may be treated with reference to cultural chronologies over a wide geographic range.

EARLY LITHIC STAGE

Cultural interconnections between North and South America, undoubtedly, began at a remote period, well before the rise of Spinden's "Archaic" or "American neolithic" stage. Middle and South American pressure-flaked points found under conditions of geological antiquity resemble certain less specialized North American point types. Wormington (1953) has noted a projectile point found in the upper Becerra formation of the Valley of Mexico as being reminiscent of the North American Scottsbluff type and another from the earliest cultural level of the Straits of Magellan as resembling the Plainview type. For the most part, Scottsbluff and Plainview points are dated somewhat later than the Clovis and Folsom types in North America. There is a radiocarbon date from a Folsom site near Lubbock, Texas (Fig. 1) which is 7932 B.C. ± 350 years.[2] The radiocarbon reading from the earliest Straits of Magellan level is a little over 1000 years later, with the exact date recorded as 6688 B.C. ± 450 years.

The data are still too few and radiocarbon dating is still too experimental to treat this subject any more definitely. However, if pressure-flaking in the New World is accepted as a diffused technique from the Old World, then the distribution of pressure-flaked tools in the Americas must have some historical connective significance within this hemisphere. Presumably, movement of both peoples and cultures in the early periods of the settlement of America was from north to south. The information available, thus, indicates intercontinental ties and even suggests a rough dating of events.

---

[2] All radiocarbon dates are from Johnson, 1951.

Fig. 1.—Sites and Cultures in Middle and South America.

In the long interval that appears to exist between the Early Lithic complexes antedating 5000 B.C. and the beginnings of maize agriculture, the cross-ties between the American continents remain of a general nature. If one assumes that such a technique as pressure-flaking of chipped stone was diffused from north to south during or at the close of the Mankato Substage of the Wisconsin glaciation, then it is difficult to deny that other industrial techniques were similarly diffused at a later time. The grinding and polishing of stone and the manufacture of polished stone objects of both utilitarian and nonutilitarian forms date from this interval in both the eastern United States Archaic[3] cultures and in similar Archaic-like contexts in California. Radiocarbon dates for these Archaic ground stone assemblages fall between 2000 and 4000 B.C. Ground stone materials occur in South America along the Brazilian and Chilean shores in shell refuse mounds which are either preceramic or nonceramic. Although the specific forms vary in all these widely separated areas, it is worthy of note that there is at least one type which is common to all. The plummet of the eastern North American Archaic, the "charmstone" of the early California horizon, the Brazilian "fusos" of the sambaquis, and the Chilean fish-line sinker are essentially the same form, an elongated, pointed stone, grooved or perforated for suspension. Not all of the cultures in this post-Early Lithic, preagricultural era, however, are associated with the making of ground and polished stone implements. The Mexican Chalco complex, which appears to fill this time gap in the Valley of Mexico, lacks such technologies and is known by its chipped stone work and rather crude grinding implements. Similarly, the earlier stages of the Arizona Cochise Culture, to which the Chalco has been compared, do not have the polished stone objects.

To sum up thus far, there is evidence for the continued exchange of stone technology between North and South America in the time interval which can be described as following the Mankato Substage of the Wisconsin glaciation (about 11,000 years ago) and extending up to perhaps 2500 B.C. Inadequate archeological sequences in South America and the absence of radiocarbon dating make it impossible to determine the exact

---

[3] It should be noted that the term "Archaic" as used in the eastern United States and in California pertains to cultures of a nonagricultural type. Spinden's use of "Archaic" is quite different, referring to the sedentary agricultural way of life designated here as Formative.

direction and time of these influences although probabilities favor a north-to-south drift. Also, there is no really solid clue as to whether these were migrations of people or diffusions of ideas. Even at this early date, there seems to have been considerable cultural diversity from area to area.

The diffusion of maize agriculture appears to have begun sometime toward the close of the era to which we have just referred. Radiocarbon dates show an early form of maize with definite pod-like characteristics appearing in the North American Southwest as early as 2500 B.C.[4] A different, but equally primitive, strain of corn has been assigned a comparable radiocarbon date in the La Perra Culture of Tamaulipas, Mexico (MacNeish, 1950, pp. 92-93). In both of these contexts, pottery is lacking and the total cultural content is such as to suggest a way of life not differing greatly from the early American hunters and gatherers. By 1359 B.C. ±250 years, according to the radiocarbon "clock," a fully developed sedentary-agricultural, pottery-making culture was under way in the Valley of Mexico. The Middle and North American data thus show primitive strains of maize at amazingly early dates and the establishment of an American Formative Period or "neolithic" in central Mexico by the middle of the second millennium B.C.

What does the South American evidence show? Bird's (1948) excavations at Huaca Prieta on the Peruvian Coast disclose a long period of non-maize, simple agriculture beginning over 2000 years B.C. Maize was introduced into this setting around 700 B.C. This first Peruvian appearance of maize coincides with the arrival of Chavín-style pottery and marks, in effect, the beginnings of a fully-developed Formative stage. These datings argue for a Middle American domestication of maize over a long time period, the rise of Formative stage cultures in Middle America, and a somewhat later diffusion of maize and Formative level culture to Peru. Obviously, the case is not closed but a South American origin for domesticated Zea mays seems much less likely than it did a few years back. At the present writing, it appears that one of the most important items in the rise of New World civilizations was diffused from north-to-south in the first millennium B.C.

---

[4] There is considerable confusion about these early Bat Cave dates. In the early reports (Mangelsdorf and Smith, 1949), Antevs' geological estimate of 2500 B.C. was accepted as conservative. A later account (Smith, 1950) shifted this to 2000 B.C. Radiocarbon dates alluded to in this same article were somewhat later, 1162 B.C. to 662 B.C. However, charcoal from the 6-foot stratum of the cave, found associated with the earliest corn, has a radiocarbon date of 3980 B.C.±310 years. In view of all these data, a medium figure of 2500 B.C. seems reasonable pending further radiocarbon runs.

When we arrive at the level of Formative culture, the criteria for detection of interarea diffusions become considerably more complex. For the Early Lithic and Archaic stages, we are utilizing stone technologies or an invention like the domestication of maize to establish common cultural bonds. But in the various Formative phases of Middle and South America there are traits whose peculiarities of form appear to afford clues to historic linkages of a more limited and intimate sort within these wider bonds. In the following discussion, I will treat with several cultural elements, or complexes of elements, selected for their definitive characteristics and for their demonstrable chronological contexts. For the most part, these selected elements will be presented in what appears to be their chronological order, from earliest to latest. As will be apparent, most of these elements are not indisputable proof of cultural contact in the same way that an actual trade object or a specific style embodies such proof. On the other hand, they have a greater specific value than a fundamental invention such as pottery-making or agriculture. They are criteria of an intermediate grade of definitiveness. Their value appears to vary with the dimensions of their space-time contexts. There is no set rule we can follow. Each instance must be examined and judged on its own merits; however, it is with these data that we must test the case for inter-American culture contacts.

Rocker-Stamped Decoration of Pottery

Rocker-stamping of pottery is a decorative technique employed on the soft, unfired surface of the vessel. It is effected with a plain or notched-edged implement manipulated in a rocker or roulette fashion. It is found in many places in the New World and also appears in Old World prehistoric contexts. Griffin and Krieger (1947) have discussed the Middle American occurrences of rocker-stamped pottery, particularly with comparative reference to the eastern United States. Strong (1943) has pointed to Peruvian similarities. More recently, Porter (1953) has reviewed the problem in the Americas suggesting that it is a diffused phenomenon. It is, of course, questionable as to just how reliable this technique may be as a historical connective. Was it invented once or many times? I am inclined to believe that rocker-stamped pottery in the New World has a common history. Beyond that, I think it an even chance that the American and the

Asiatic occurrences are also remotely related. In the New World, the most interesting fact concerning this decorative technique on pottery is that it is almost uniformly early. It appears in the Formative Stage periods of Middle America and Peru and has a respectable antiquity in the eastern United States, giving an excellent illustration of chronological context strengthening the diffusional hypothesis.

By using the ceramic decorative technique of rocker-stamping as a tracer, we arrive at the following construct for Middle America and Andean South America. First, the technique appears on the Mexican scene between 1000 and 500 B.C. It is associated with Upper Formative cultures in central Mexico, Veracruz, and in the Atlantic drainages of Honduras. It occurs in north lowland Colombia where it is early in a relative sense (Reichel-Dolmatoff, 1954). In north Peru, it is associated with the appearance of maize and the first "full blown" Formative type cultures (Chavín and Cupisnique) at around 700 B.C. Comparative dates at the Mexican and Peruvian ends of the chart are approximately the same and give no good clue to the direction of diffusion. However, the cultural milieu into which rocker-stamping first appears in Middle America is considerably richer and deeper than that for Peru where the technique is known only from Chavín horizon. Such a consideration favors a north-south movement of the technique. Further, we know that rocker-stamping is an ancient pottery technique in Asia, placed by some authorities at 2000 B.C. in Mongolia-Manchuria (Liang, 1930). In Ohio and Illinois, rocker-stamped pottery reaches its climax in the Middle Hopewellian period at around 300 to 0 B.C. according to recent radiocarbon dates, but it has a long previous history in those regions according to some authorities (Griffin, 1952) which may well carry the technique back to dates equivalent with or earlier than those of Middle and South America. In the light of these facts, it is by no means an unfounded speculation that rocker-stamping as a pottery technique entered the eastern United States from Asia, was diffused southward to the lowlands of eastern Mexico, and continued in that general direction through Honduras, Colombia, and Ecuador into Peru.

It should be pointed out that this technique fits into a remarkably similar context in both Mexico and Peru. Traits common to Tlatilco in Mexico and Coastal Chavín in Peru include such elements as incised color zones in pottery decoration, stirrup-spouted vessels, pottery stamps, whistling jars, a jaguar motif, and a curious concept of dualism as artistic representations. Some of these traits, but not all of them, are associated with the other Middle American occurrences of rocker-stamped pottery. Many are features which continue until much later times in both areas. The stirrup-spouted jar trait continues in post-Chavín periods in north Peru to become

35

one of the most common pottery forms; in Middle America it is always a minor element. Conversely, pottery stamps disappear in the later Peruvian periods but remain a common Middle American artifact. In connection with this, we observe that in some of the interlying regions, such as Colombia, both stirrup-spouted jars and pottery stamps are significant elements in most archeological complexes.

Platform Mounds

In the Valley of Mexico, platform mounds date from the late Upper Formative Stage phases, such as Cuicuilco. In the Maya lowlands, a small platform like A-I at Uaxactun also appears in the Upper Formative. The stepped pyramid (E-VII-sub) at Uaxactun is either late Formative or belongs to the succeeding Early Classic phase. In Yucatan, mound building appears in the latter part of the Formative (Brainerd, 1951, p. 76). In the lowlands of the Gulf Coast of Mexico, platform or substructure mounds are found in the Veracruz-Tabasco region, and in every instance the relative sequence position is the Upper Formative Period or later. In Honduras, large platform mounds were constructed in association with a complex which, from all indications, belongs on this same general time level. Only in the Guatemala highlands is there any substantial evidence indicating an earlier position for the flat-topped pyramid or platform mound. There, puddled adobe mounds came into the sequence during the Arevalo phase (personal communication, A. V. Kidder and E. M. Shook) which is, unfortunately, not satisfactorily cross-dated to other Middle American sequences. However, there is at least the possibility that it may be Lower rather than Upper Formative.

In Peru, the earliest platform mounds are Chavín horizon structures in Cupisnique, Nepeña, and Casma Valleys. Their appearance on the north coast of Peru coincides with the introduction of rocker-stamped pottery and maize agriculture, and marks the beginning of the Peruvian Formative Stage. Radiocarbon dating places this period in Peru approximately contemporary with the earliest platform mounds in the Middle American Upper Formative period.[5]

This chronological coincidence would appear to signify another interrelationship between Peru and Middle America on about the same time level as that of the presumed diffusion of rocker-stamped pottery. The counter-possibility of the independent development of large ceremonial

---

[5] This correlation is essentially the same as that presented by Wauchope (1954) in his "Scheme A."

structures in Peru and in Middle America deserves more consideration here, however, than in the case of rocker-stamping. Mound building is directly tied to population concentration and organization; the rocker-stamped marking of pottery is not. In examining the independent developmental hypothesis, it may be significant to observe that whereas platform mounds do not occur in Middle America until well after the start of Formative sedentary-agricultural life, they are part of the Peruvian Formative at its inception. Of course, if the phenomena are independent of each other, this could have resulted from an acceleration of population growth on the Peruvian coast; however, it also suggests the other interpretation—that the platform mound was diffused to Peru from Middle America where it is underlaid by a longer Formative heritage.

The distribution of the platform mound in the intervening areas of lower Central America, Colombia, and Ecuador throws little light on the problems of diffusion. In general, substructure mounds decrease in size and numbers through Nicaragua, Costa Rica, and Panama. Relative dates are as yet unavailable from these regions, so there is no proof that mounds were built on a time level corresponding to the Formative of either Middle America or Peru. In Colombia, there is little clear evidence of large mounds although small tumuli are reported from various sections of the country. In some instances these tumuli may be substructures, but in others, they seem to have served only as burial places. Temple or palace platform mounds are common in Ecuador, particularly along the coast and slightly inland from the coast. The Ecuadorian chronologies are sketchy, at best, and cannot be securely tied to the north Peruvian sequences; however, there is a fair possibility that the platform-mound trait on the Ecuadorian coast may be as early as the Peruvian Formative period. In reviewing the distributional evidence, the weakest link is seen in Colombia. This Colombian link, or lack of a link, is an argument against the diffusion of the platform mound idea; however, it is quite possible that the Colombia area was by-passed in such a diffusion. As will be noted farther along, there are a number of other curious similarities between Peru and Middle America and between Ecuador and Middle America that are not registered in Colombia.

Resist-Dye Painting of Pottery

This pottery technique has sometimes been referred to as negative-painting or "lost-color" painting, but the term "resist-dye" probably approximates the actual techniques used most closely. Pottery decorated by this technique was apparently treated in somewhat the same manner as batik-processed textiles. Certain design areas were blocked out by a wax, gum, or other resist material and the vessel was then immersed in, or covered with, the over-coat dye or paint. Upon firing or cleaning of the surface, the design then stood out in the lighter under-color of the original slip or surface color while the background to these designs was blocked out in the darker (usually blackish) dye. As can be seen, the process possesses a certain complexity that makes it suitable as a tracer in diffusion studies.

In Middle America, resist-dye pottery has a late or Upper Formative occurrence in the central Mexican regions and in Maya lowlands. In Guatemala, Salvador, and Honduras, a ware known as Usulutan appears to have been decorated by a resist technique. There is some dispute about the Usulutan technique but its appearance impresses me as a resist or negative ware, not unlike the various resist-dye pottery styles of Peru, Ecuador, Colombia, and Central America. There are several instances of both Usulutan and other resist-dye potteries continuing after the late Formative level into Classic times; but only in highland Guatemala does there seem to be an earlier beginning. In brief, resist-dye painted pottery in Middle America is mainly a feature of the Upper Formative and occurs contemporaneously with, or slightly later than, rocker-stamped pottery.

In Peru, resist-dye pottery, more commonly known in this area as negative-painted pottery, is best known from the north highlands and the north coast. The over-all time position of the technique is best summarized by saying that it has its Peruvian inception immediately following the Chavín horizon, and perhaps, overlapping slightly with that horizon. Using the Coast Chavín radiocarbon date of about 700 B.C. as a base line, the beginnings of Peruvian resist-dye painting on pottery lie somewhere in the three or four centuries following this date. This is approximately the same temporal position as in Middle America, with the possible exception of the early Usulutan occurrences at the site of Kaminaljuyu, Guatemala.

There is little upon which to base a guess as to the direction of the diffusion of the resist-dye technique. As far as abundance and elaboration of resist-dye wares are concerned, north Peru and Ecuador is undoubtedly a center. Resist-dye painted pottery enjoys a vogue northward through the Nariño and Quimbaya regions of Colombia and is a major element in the Chiriquí pottery of Panama and Costa Rica. Presumably, the latter styles are relatively late chronologically but little is known as yet of earlier archeological periods in these regions. For the present, the case for a diffusion of the resist-dye painting technique on pottery between Middle America and Peru is based upon mutually early and approximately contemporaneous occurrences in each area. The diversity of distribution of the technique suggests a South American hearth, but this gives no real assurance of chronological priority.

Mold-Made Figurines

Mold-made figurines first appear in the central Mexican sequence in Early Classic times. They are preceded in that region by a long and continuous Formative tradition of hand-made figurines. In the Maya area, the earliest mold-made figurines have been placed at somewhere between 500 and 800 A.D. (Butler, 1935). The inferred diffusion is from central Mexico southward inasmuch as the tradition of figurine-making was missing from the Maya lowlands following the Early Formative level. The obvious implication is that figurines were reintroduced, along with the technology of the mold, from Classic Teotihuacan or closely related cultures of central Mexico. This general dating of mold-made figurines in the Classic Period is consistent for the rest of Middle America.

In Peru, the mold was used for figurines for the first time in the Mochica Culture of the north coast of Peru. It is possible that molds were used earlier for the manufacture of some pottery vessels, but there is no evidence as yet for an earlier application of the figurine mold. There is some indication that the Mochica Culture lasted over a considerable span of centuries and it is not as yet possible to place the mold-made figurine trait within this span. In the central and southern highlands of Peru, the mold and mold-made figurines are less common than on the north coast, and there is every indication they are also later than in the north.

A comparison of radiocarbon dates in Middle America and Peru suggests that the invention of the figurine mold was older in Peru than in Middle America. As opposed to this, the deep tradition of hand-made figurine manufacture in Middle America, which antedates the use of the mold, is an argument for a Middle American origin of this trait. A crucial datum in this matter is the presence of a highly developed, mold-made figurine industry on the north coast of Ecuador. This industry centers around Esmeraldas, but related figurine types are found farther south as well. The Esmeraldas style of figurines and figurine plaques (D'Harcourt, 1947) shows similarities to Mochica figurines and to Mochica relief-modeled erotica on pottery. At the same time, other Esmeraldas types resemble Middle American mold-made figurines, especially those from the Veracruz lowlands (Bushnell, 1951) and the Colima-Nayarit styles of the Mexican west coast (Lehmann, 1951). From this, it seems at least a likely possibility that sea-faring Ecuadorean coastal cultures may have served as intermediaries in transmitting certain figurine concepts and the ceramic mold technology between the Mexicans and the Peruvians. Chronological studies on the development of figurines in the Esmeraldas region are needed to check such a hypothesis.

The Tall Tripod Pottery Vessel

Up to now, the traits discussed in this Middle American-Peruvian comparison have appeared to assemble on chronological horizon lines. The radiocarbon dates have indicated that certain elements made their initial appearance in Middle America at about the same time that they are first noted in Peru. Undoubtedly, this is an over-simplified appraisal and we are not trying to skip over contradictory data. The rather early radio-carbon date for Mochica Culture in Peru (Strong and Evans, 1952, foot-note p. 226) and possibly for the figurine mold is one such exception which does not fit the horizon picture. Nevertheless, rocker-stamping, resist-dye painting, and mold-made figurines succeed one another in reasonable chronological regularity in both Middle America and Peru. There are, however, certain elements which violate even the broadest time horizons but which, in spite of this, offer clues to cultural connections. One of these is the tall, solid, tripod support to a pottery vessel.

There are a variety of vessel supports in Middle American archeology. The earliest form seems to be a small, hollow tripod foot which appears in the Lower Formative of the Valley of Mexico. Podal supports are more common in the Upper Formative and include a variety of hollow forms as well as small, solid, nubbin feet. What appears to be a late Upper Formative or Proto-Classic horizon marker in parts of Middle America is the large mammiform support (Wauchope, 1950). Tall, solid, tripod supports are less common in Middle America than some of these other forms, but they appear at the beginning of the Upper Formative. Similar tall, solid, tripod supports are reported in highland 'Guatemala but here they come into the sequence in the Early Formative. The trait thus has considerable antiquity in Middle American cultures.

The Peruvian pottery tripod is almost exclusively a Post-Classic fea-ture, occurring with and after the Tiahuanaco horizon. Certainly, this is true of the tall, solid-legged variety, which most closely resembles the Mexican and Guatemalan form (King, 1948). All estimated dating would indicate that the tall tripod element does not occur in Peru until almost 1000 A.D., perhaps 1500 to 2000 years after its Middle American appear-ance. Such a tremendous slope leaves little doubt as to the direction from which the tall tripod idea was spread to Peru. There is, of course, no definite proof that the invention is a Middle American one. The tall tripod is a pottery trait of the Colombian-Ecuadorian regions and although an antiquity for the tripod in these regions comparable to that of Guatemala or Mexico cannot be demonstrated as yet, it is quite possible that tripod supports were an important part of Ecuadorean ceramics well before the Tiahuanaco horizon in Peru. It would seem that either the tall tripod idea was diffused south from Middle America into Colombia and Ecuador, where it was retained for a considerable time before being transmitted to Peru, or the tall tripod had its origins in Colombia-Ecuador and diffused in both directions, reaching Middle America far earlier than Peru.

Metallurgy

Metallurgy, like the tall tripod, describes a "sloping horizon" in its Middle American-Peruvian space-time distribution. It differs from the tripods in that it slopes the other way. American metallurgical techniques were first developed in South America, some of them possibly in Peru. The earliest annealing and soldering, in addition to cold hammering and repoussé designing, belong to the Coast Chavín horizon and come from the Chongoyape graves in the Lambayeque Valley of the north Peruvian coast. Gold was the primary metal used, with small bits of silver in association. It is possible that this represents technical influences diffused into Peru from Ecuador or from Colombia via Ecuador. There is, however, no proof of this diffusion, and Lothrop (1951, pp. 223) feels that this earliest Peruvian metallurgy was a local development.

There was little advance in Peruvian metals following the Chavín horizon until Gallinazo times, which mark the close of the Formative and the beginning of north coast Classic culture. Copper was introduced in the Gallinazo period and the techniques of casting, gilding, and overlaying were added to those already known. In the subsequent Mochica period, alloying and casting were widely employed, *tumbaga* (an alloy of gold and copper) was known, and metal (copper) was used for the first time on the north coast for weapons and tools. Lothrop (1951) believes that *tumbaga, cire perdue* (lost wax) casting, and *mise-en-couleur* gilding moved into Peru on this level from centers in Colombia such as the Quimbaya region. This is certainly a possibility but, again, lack of Ecuadorian-Colombian sequence data makes a diffusion from Peru northward an equally good possibility. The central and southern regions of Peru seem to have been remote from this northern orbit of the development of metals, and

41

the early south coast and south highland centers show little in the way of metallurgical skill. During Classic Tiahuanaco times, however, the south highlands appear to have become an important secondary metallurgical center where bronze was developed. In the subsequent Tiahuanaco horizon, and in the late kingdoms and the Inca empire, bronze tools, weapons, and other artifacts were widely diffused throughout Peru. Bronze reached Ecuador on the Inca horizon.

With regard to Ecuador, it is certain that metals and metallurgical techniques, including the use of copper tools and axes, were known on a time level equivalent to that of Peruvian Mochica. Whether these crafts antedate their appearance in Peru or are a result of Peruvian stimulus, is still an open question.

There is every indication that cast gold and *tumbaga* and gilded metal objects were a relatively late introduction in such cultures as Veraguas and Coclé in Panama. Northward, metals were unknown in the Maya area until very late Classic times (about 900 to 1000 A.D.) and then they appear as foreign manufactures. The Middle American center for metal work was along the Mexican southwest coast in late Post-Classic times. Some of the objects found here are strikingly like those of Ecuador and Peru, particularly the axes and the copper ax form used as a medium of exchange. These similarities point to direct Ecuadorian-Mexican contact by sea as they are not shared by the intermediate Colombian and lower Central American regions.

Miscellaneous Late Traits

The northward diffusion of metallurgy into Middle America at what was almost certainly a late period brings to mind a number of other late examples, which indicate that a vigorous coast-wise trade was in operation. I believe it likely that the Ecuadorian coastal trading cities of late prehistoric times, such as the center of Manta, were the principal agents by which this commerce was carried out. The Manteño were skilled navigators and occupied a favorable geographic position to have served as middle men between the Aztec, Mixtec, and Guatemalan tribes in the north and the Chimu kingdom of Peru. In addition to copper axes and metallurgy, occasional objects have been found which show definite linkages in one direction or the other. A pottery seal picked up on the Ecuadorean coast bears a design incorporating a speech-scroll feature and, although made locally and in a local style, the speech-scroll element is a highly specific Mexican feature (Brainerd, 1953). On the Pacific Coast of Guatemala, a pottery vessel of the Peruvian Coast Tiahuanaco kero-form, bearing a painted Nazca style fish design, is an element from the other direction (Disseldorf, 1933, pl. 53, fig. 141). Also, there are the Chimu-like vessels which Lothrop has reported from Zacualpa, Guatemala (1936, fig. 92) and from Panama (1942, fig. 440). These are either actual trade pieces or local imitations. Then there are the rather startling design similarities between the stone wall mosaics of Mitla in Oaxaca, Mexico, and the arabesques of Peruvian north coastal cities like Chan Chan. All of these features are isolated in themselves, clearly not a part of any cultural complex which has been transferred *en toto;* but such indeed is expectable if they were transmitted and reproduced through the random impressions of traders and voyagers.

CONCLUSIONS

What can we conclude concerning the case for culture contact between prehistoric Middle America and South America? Let us summarize the evidence in a series of major time bands. First, the earliest human occupations of South America equate chronologically, and to some extent typologically, with the North American lithic complexes which follow the Folsom horizon and appear to date between 7500 and 5000 B.C. The mutual traits are few, but hunting cultures in both continents share flint chipping technologies and certain projectile point forms. In spite of the lack of complex evidence, a relationship between these cultures of the Early Lithic Stage is indicated since from where else could ideas of stone work have entered South America except from North America?

The second time band, extending perhaps from 5000 to 2500 B.C. and here called the Archaic Stage, is characterized by the rather general traits of stone grinding, carving, and polishing. Occasional forms from South and North America are similar but these are not the crux of the argument. Again, from where else could these technologies in South America have been diffused except from North America? It is somewhere near the upper range of this second time band that domesticated maize is found in northeastern Middle America and in the southwestern United States. No maize with radiocarbon dates anywhere near this early has been discovered in the southern continent.

The third time band may be approximated as from 2500 B.C. to the beginning of the Christian era. This corresponds to the Formative Stage cultures characterized by the establishment of sedentary, agricultural, village life in both Middle America and Peru. The earliest actual dates are in Mexico where the bottom of the Formative column of cultural phases is placed at 1350 B.C. Middle American culture at this time was well advanced in the ceramic arts. The evidences for specific lines of diffusion between Middle America and Peru within this time band assemble on a chronological level of about 800 to 400 B.C. They include the technique of rocker-stamped decoration on pottery, the construction of platform mounds, and the technique of resist-dye painting of pottery. The last of these traits may be slightly later than the other two. One of the most interesting facts emerging from these correlations is that rocker-stamped pottery and the platform mound seem to appear in Peru simultaneously, and that their appearance is also synchronized with the earliest finds of domesticated maize. The Peruvian cultures antedating these appearances or arrivals were definitely of a sub-Formative type. These circumstances suggest a significant diffusion of "neolithic" traits from Middle to South America at a time corresponding to the beginning of the Middle American Upper Formative cultures. Although this does not correspond in all specifics to the various theories of Uhle, Jijón y Caamaño, and Spinden as regards the fundamental agricultural-pottery-making diffusions from Middle to South America, it tends to confirm the general structure of their hypotheses. Resist-dye painting may be a reverse diffusion from Peru back to Middle America, although we cannot be sure of this. The respective dates for the inception of the trait in the two areas are about the same.

A fourth time band lies somewhere between 1 A.D. and 1000 A.D. and corresponds roughly to the periods of the Classic cultures in both Peru and Middle America. I have selected the mold-made figurine as the key element of this time band. The principle is a technological one, and the figurines themselves show no close stylistic correspondence although certain Ecuadorean specimens are reminiscent of both Mexican and Peruvian designs. 'The historical connective value of the trait is assumed to lie in the technological process itself, the use of the mold to produce the pottery image. The direction of diffusion is questionable. Mochica radiocarbon dates from Peru are earlier than the dates imputed to Teotihuacan III in Mexico but the long tradition of figurine-making in Middle America, antecedent to the appearance of the mold, tends to favor a Middle American origin.

A fifth time band runs from 1000 A.D. to the Spanish conquests of the early 16th century. We have noted a number of miscellaneous items here such as the pottery seal with the speech scroll design from the Ecuadorean coast and the Peruvian-like pottery specimens from Guatemala. Intersecting into this fifth time band are the traits of tall tripod vessels and of metallurgy. Both have a diagonal or "sloping" horizon conformation on the time chart. The tall tripod is definitely early (appearing in the

Formative) in Middle America and late (Post-Classic) in Peru; and metal-lurgy, which has a Formative stage occurrence in Peru, does not reach Middle America until about 1000 A.D. or later. In connection with this latter trait complex, it has been noted that the center for Mexican metal-craft is the southwest coast of Mexico, a region which shows other evidences of contact with the Ecuadorean and Peruvian coasts. Sea trade between Ecuador and Mexico seems the most likely explanation of these particular phenomena.

This discussion has been directed toward establishing a case for culture contact between Middle America and Peru during the prehistoric past. I have dealt with a selected number of traits and have tried to show how these traits may be organized in space and in time so that the historical possibilities of diffusion may be demonstrated. To my mind, there seems little doubt that various contacts took place, some indirectly and others, per-haps, more directly. Accepting the currently available radiocarbon dates, a definite case may be made for the priority of American Formative type cul-tures in Middle America and their subsequent influencing of Peru. As stated at the outset, I have made no attempt to interpret the cultural and develop-mental significance of the traits discussed or, with the exception of casual references, to draw inferences as to the means or processes by which such ancient contacts and diffusions were accomplished. Almost certainly, con-tact of one sort or another was maintained from remote Early Lithic times down to the end of an autonomous native America. What it meant in the various American areas and how it played a part in cultural acceleration and change is an infinitely more complex story than the one I have sketchily outlined here.

TRENDS IN SOUTHWESTERN ARCHEOLOGY

Erik K. Reed

FOR ABOUT 20 years, roughly 1930 to 1950, Southwestern archeology has gone through a period which may be called one of fragmentation—of analysis and taxonomy, of classification into units as small as possible, both in detail (notably the separation and naming of pottery types on the basis of any recognizable distinctions) and on a broader scale in the demarcation of cleavages between cultural sequences of several areas in the Southwest. Emphasis has been largely placed on differentiation between groups or complexes rather than on general underlying or cross-cutting unities. Description of small cultural units (foci or phases) and branches (local sequences, series of foci), and of pottery types (of other artifacts to a far less degree) has been the main effort. Of the several differing groups detectable in the Southwest, at least four have been called cultures, roots, or basic cultures.

More than 25 years ago, at the Conference held at Pecos Pueblo in 1927, the first systematic period classification for Southwestern archeology was worked out (Kidder, 1927); it is still extensively used, though generally with modifications in period designations offered later by Roberts (1935). Very shortly, workers entering the hitherto little-studied southern part of the Southwest realized that the Pecos Classification could not be satisfactorily applied in the Gila Basin and, further, that they were dealing with material quite different from that of the San Juan region on which the Pecos Classification had been largely based and which had been thought of as the typical and nuclear area of the Southwest. A conference at Globe in 1931 set up the "Hohokam" of southern Arizona as a distinct culture with a quite separate period classification (Fig. 2).

A few years later another portion of the Southwest was split off from the San Juan-Pecos development, which now began to be called by the special term "Anasazi." In 1933-34, the late H. P. Mera (1934) recognized the "Southern Brownware complex" in the Petrified Forest district

46

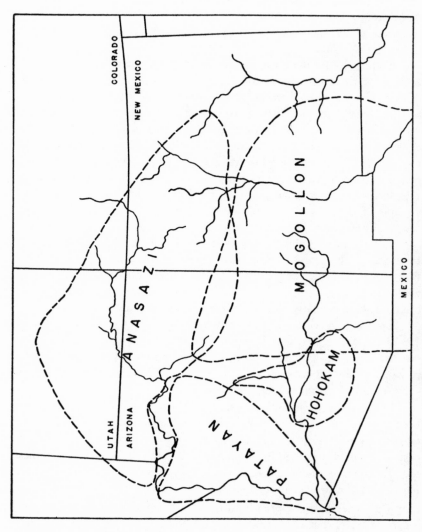

Fig. 2.—Distribution of Major Archeological Cultures in the Southwest.

of Arizona (Fig. 3) and southward, and Gladwin and Haury set off the "Mogollon Culture" in southwestern New Mexico as being separate both from the Hohokam of southern Arizona and the San Juan Anasazi or typical Pueblo of the northern Southwest. Both were referring to the same basic group. The term "Mogollon" was taken up and widely applied to materials all the way from southeastern New Mexico to the Verde Valley in central Arizona.

Colton, during the same period, had begun to perceive, in his detailed analysis of the archeological remains in the vicinity of Flagstaff in north-central Arizona, that three or more distinct elements were involved, had met and mixed in that district. Among these the "Kayenta branch" was unquestionably Pueblo, and clearly San Juan Anasazi specifically; the "Sinagua branch" and other local groups were not. A colony of Hohokam from the Verde Valley was found in McGregor's (1941) work at Winona, elements of Mogollon affiliation were recognized, and also still different materials in certain respects suggestive of the little-known Yuman archeological remains of the Lower Colorado River. Colton (1938; 1939) suggested a fourth distinct root or basic culture to include these last, the "Patayan."

There was a certain amount of resistance to the subdivision and splitting, and to the analytical approach generally. As late as 1940, and to a degree even after the war, the Mogollon Culture was occasionally referred to as illegitimate, peripheral, hybrid, or transitional, and the Patayan root often has been similarly handled or even completely ignored.

But the trend certainly was overwhelmingly as described from the early 1930's on; and it has been a highly desirable and valuable one, spreading out the material, dividing it up and sorting it into the smallest categories possible, producing the detailed analysis on which any sound and successful generalized synthesis must be based.

In the post-war years, however, a contrary trend has been observable, becoming conspicuous recently—an expectable development and normal reaction from the classificatory approach. It may be regarded as an exploitation of the data presented in the detailed breakdowns, to seek the synthesis for the sake of which these analyses were produced. To support and improve it, of course, continued analytical work is needed.

The generalizing approach, the trend to synthesis, has two distinct aspects. One is that of setting up broad general periods for a large part of the entire area, successive cultural stages cross cutting the local sequences and each embracing foci or periods of several branches. Two rather similar such presentations have been outlined in the last two years, the "Southwestern co-tradition" of Martin and Rinaldo (1951) and the "New conceptual scheme" of Daifuku (1952). In these frameworks, we find (1) an

48

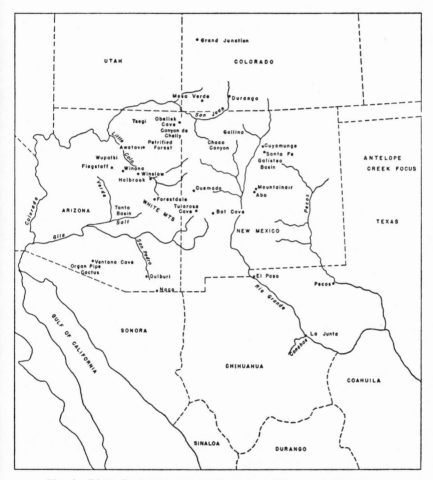

Fig. 3.—River Drainages and Archeological Sites in the Southwest.

Elementary Southwestern Stage, or Pre-agricultural and Early agricultural, with B.C. dates; (2) a Formative Stage during most of the first millenium of the Christian era; (3) a Florescent or Classic Stage in which a peak of cultural development and population density was reached; and (4) the Fusion Period in the late pre-Spanish and early historic times, corresponding to Pueblo IV of the Pecos Classification. With adjustments and corrections, and continuing modifications as new additional data become available, a descriptive outline of this kind will undoubtedly become accepted and generally used.

Along with this generalizing approach on a horizontal principle, there has also appeared considerable synthesis on vertical lines. By this I mean attempts to trace historical sequences of development, of cultural traditions, and actual population lineages from earliest visible beginnings through into historic times and to connect them up with specific modern Indian tribes. This "vertical" approach is, obviously, an attempt at the reconstruction of human history which is the first objective of archeological work and has also the incidental advantage of relating the much-classified and analyzed specimens of archeology to actual living people. The "historical" grouping of the materials in general periods representing successive levels of cultural development, if it can be done satisfactorily, has, perhaps, broader implications for progress in theory and philosophy of human history and general cultural anthropology.

Another significant and valuable development in Southwestern archeology in recent years has been the continuing expansion of interest and activity into the "peripheries"—areas largely omitted in the period schemes mentioned above—out from the Rio Grande, San Juan and Gila basins into the desert areas of western Arizona, where Schroeder's yet largely unpublished material provides much new information on Yuman prehistory; into Nevada and Utah (Rudy and Stirland, 1950); to La Junta on the Rio Grande at the other extreme, where Kelley has done extremely valuable work; in eastern New Mexico, where similarities to the Antelope Creek Culture of the Texas Panhandle are recognized; and on the western slope in Colorado, north of the Southwest proper as commonly pictured or defined, where Wormington, Lister, and others have made very interesting finds of Southwestern affiliation, around Grand Junction and as far north as the Yampa, with pottery of Southwestern types being found clear up in southwestern Wyoming and even Idaho.

With continuing active systematic work in Utah under Jennings' direction, with more work in western Arizona (such as Ezell's recent survey of the Organ Pipe Cactus district south of Ajo) and in southern Nevada, with more attention to Southwest-southern California connections, and with the increasing interest in Plains-Southwest relationships, all of our borders are in fairly good shape except to the south, the most important direction.

The findings of Ekholm and others in northwestern Mexico have helped greatly but large gaps yet remain. More work in Sonora and Chihuahua is probably the outstanding single need of Southwestern archeology now, as it has been for years. Lister has recently worked in Chihuahua with most promising results and a major stride has been taken toward filling in the lack by Kelley in working up the Conchos River from La Junta, in southern Chihuahua and into Durango, and in determining there, at least tentatively, the dividing-line or meeting-point between Mexican and Southwestern cultures. H. A. Carey of Morehead, Kentucky, is working on Chihuahua sites along the New Mexico border, and still other investigations in several states of northern Mexico are in progress or planned.

In fine, the recent progress of Southwestern archeology has been considerable and the present status of the study is a highly encouraging though temporarily muddled condition of moving from a period of constant revision and reanalysis and of separatism and taxonomic detail into a stage of crystallization and synthesis, of pulling the pieces back together into a general historical picture and its 'cultural-anthropological interpretation. With a sharpening sense of problem and increasing interest in historical continuities being manifested, and with studies perhaps less channeled away from research planning by urgent River Basin demands and other salvage needs elsewhere, we are on the verge of sketching the outlines of Southwestern prehistory fairly definitely, and of going on into ecological and anthropological explanations of the phenomena observed—beginning to determine what happened, we have now to decide how and why it happened.

Rather than essaying to summarize here the entire outline of prehistoric trends and events which I have rashly claimed is already emerging from the welter of data and details, I shall next mention some of the more significant recent developments which have materially changed our conception of the story.

In chronological order (of original happening, not of finding) the first item is the Naco mammoth (Haury, 1953) on the Arizona-Sonora border—the first definite recovery of early (Clovis Fluted) points in the Southwest proper, west of the High Plains region. We know from this major find (made only in 1951-52) that the Upper Paleolithic early American hunters did enter the Southwest at least 10,000 years ago.

Considerable additional material has been accumulated on the Cochise complex in southern Arizona and southwestern New Mexico which may be called, or at least compared to, the Mesolithic and typified as general food collecting, as against earlier primary dependence upon hunting of big game. The most important single site would be Ventana Cave in south-western Arizona, excavated in 1940-42 (Haury, 1950), where major con-nections westward with southern California and Folsom-like elements link the Cochise Culture more firmly with other early developments. Radio-carbon dates have been obtained supporting Antevs' (1941) dating of the Cochise stages—the first, Sulphur Springs, 5805 and 4260 B.C. (Antevs: 8000 B.C.); the second, Chiricahua, 2550 and 2050 B.C. (Antevs: 3000 B.C.); and San Pedro, around 500 B.C.

By far the most important single revolutionary change is the finding in Bat Cave (Dick, 1952) and Tularosa Cave (Martin and Rinaldo, 1952) in southwestern New Mexico of maize, going back far earlier in the Cochise sequence than had been imagined—at Bat Cave at least to 1000 B.C., pos-sibly to a period between 5000 and 2500 B.C. Other food crops, beans and squash, apparently were present by a time between 300 and 150 B.C. as found in Tularosa Cave. The surprising antiquity of maize in the South-west calls for a radical change of historical interpretation, although other areas (not only southern Mexico but also the Mississippi-southeastern United States, according to radiocarbon dates) were already far ahead of the Southwest in cultural advancement during the first millennium B.C.

Pit houses appear in the San Pedro horizon of the Cochise Culture in the south, datable between 500 B.C. and 200 B.C., and by 200 A.D. in the northern Southwest (at Basket Maker sites near Durango, Colorado). Pottery making was introduced from Mexico in the southern area, trans-forming Cochise into Mogollon, by about 150 B.C., spread thence into eastern-central Arizona (320 A.D. at Forestdale and well before 500 A.D. in the Petrified Forest area) and finally, by 475 A.D., as shown at Obelisk Cave, reached the San Juan Anasazi (Basket Makers) of the Four Corners region. The bow and arrow, apparently, reached the Mogollon people well before 500 A.D., the Anasazi somewhat after that time. In the Hohokam area of the Gila Basin, a distinctive cultural development meanwhile began to diverge from the Mogollon group, again with pottery, the bow and arrow, and other new traits added to a Cochise base.

The foregoing paragraph is based upon so many finds and concepts that it has to be given as straight narrative and flat statement; I believe it would all be generally accepted—and it is rather different from, or at least more definite than, what we might have said a few years back.

For one thing, the dichotomy between Mogollon and Anasazi has become almost universally recognized; the only serious question on this now is whether to call both groups "Pueblo" or to continue restricting that rather general term only to the Anasazi (or to the later phases thereof which are distinguished by artificial cranial deformation). Personally, I am against segregation, even separate but equal recognition.

A change of major importance in the picture of Anasazi history in the San Juan region was brought about, within the past 20 years, primarily by a few physical anthropologists. The "broad-headed" and "more mongoloid" Pueblo folk, supposed to have arrived in the 700's bringing virtually no important new cultural elements except perhaps the bow and arrow, absorbing the "Basket Makers" and carrying forward their tradition, was found upon careful examination to be mythical; no such invasion occurred. The alleged change in physical type was caused by the rapid spread of the practice of artificial occipital deformation, whether deliberate for its own sake or produced unintentionally by the use of a hard cradleboard. The gradual recognition, from 1936 to 1946, of Anasazi continuity in population as well as in culture, necessitated major readjustments in our thinking.

In the same 10-year period, the idea that the Mogollon people were non-Pueblo in physical type was published, considered, and finally discarded.

The idea that the Mogollon Culture disappeared as such in developing into Mimbres, Tularosa, Cibola-Salado, and other classic-period manifestations; that the Mogollon people were overrun and submerged by a great wave of Anasazi influence and even actual people from the north, appears to be losing ground slightly. As I have pointed out before, the only two major Anasazi traits constituting this alleged overwhelming surge are the very conspicuous items of black-on-white pottery and surface masonry pueblos. These are not, however, accompanied in the south by the really distinctive Anasazi features of gray corrugated utility pottery and circular kivas.

In fact, it is possible to recognize and trace in general terms two major cultural traditions, both Puebloan in a fairly specific sense and both carried by people of the Southwest Plateau racial type, the Mogollon and the Anasazi paralleling each other through a long period; with interchange and mutual influence and with interpenetration and transitional or mixed groups, but maintaining actually a remarkable degree of separateness through a long period of time.

The distinctive traits of the San Juan Anasazi include: gray utility pottery (accompanied primarily by black-on-white painted, in some areas by an orange ware sequence which includes red-slipped types); masonry pueblos with circular kivas; the full-grooved stone axe; the lambdoid type of artificial cranial deformation. Pueblo groups of Mogollon derivation are characterized by polished brownware (plain, smudged, red-slipped, cor-

53

rugated yet polished, and painted; accompanied by black-on-white, in many districts and periods, as well as by red-on-brown, black-on-red, and polychrome types); pueblos with rectangular kivas, or none; the $\frac{3}{4}$-grooved polished stone axe; vertical occipital deformation.

There is, of course, a zone of transition rather than a sharp boundary between these two. Along the Little Colorado, particularly in the vicinity of Winslow and Holbrook, it is not well-known. In western-central New Mexico, however, what was a few years ago the largest blank space in the Southwestern archeological map is being filled in, between the Puerco and the Upper Gila and between the Rio Grande and the Zuni country, by the Peabody Museum of Harvard University expeditions in the Quemado area and by Ruppe and Dittert in the Acoma country.

On the west, continued investigations and studies in the Sinagua province of the Flagstaff-Wupatki district and the Verde Valley have led to detailed knowledge of the main phases of Sinagua Culture and to a hypothesis with far-reaching implications. In the view propounded by Schroeder (1947), the Sinagua people originally were not Pueblo (Mogollon) at all but were basically of Patayan affiliation, picking up a number of Mogollon, Anasazi, and Hohokam traits; they appear to have expanded southward in the 1100's through the Verde Valley to the Salt River valley replacing or submerging the Hohokam who previously occupied those areas.

With further thinking along this line, and some new additional information, it has begun to seem very possible that another concept first set forth about 25 years ago will vanish or at least be profoundly modified— that of the "Salado" people coming down out of the mountains to the Tonto Basin about 1200, then into the Gila-Salt River basin about 1300 and living side by side with Hohokam but maintaining their identity, then moving upstream and finally disappearing or perhaps returning northward. On closer examination, this entire circular migration of a supposedly distinct people is far less clear and certain than has been assumed, and may prove to be essentially the spread through time and space of a single conspicuous pottery type, Gila Polychrome.

Most important of all recent developments is the brilliant work in southeastern Arizona of DiPeso, who has closed the gap—or, rather, eliminated the alleged gap—between archeology and history by tying pre-Spanish remains to historically-known Piman Indian tribes and indicating that Gila Polychrome may have been, like several other important pottery types in the north, manufactured over a long period of time. This has a number of important effects which have not yet been fully felt. For one thing, it means that the presumed date of 1400 to 1450 for abandonment

of large areas in Arizona, based upon logical but actually unreliable negative evidence, no longer holds.

Nevertheless, by the coming of the first Spaniards in 1540, the Pueblos
had been reduced to approximately their modern distribution—the Hopi
and Zuni groups, Acoma, and the Rio Grande province (including, from
before 1540 to about 1680, the Piro district south of Isleta and around
Mountainair, and other smaller groups, or large individual sites like Pecos,
abandoned since 1680). Exactly why this happened is uncertain, especially
as regards the abandonment of the entire San Juan drainage about 1300.
The debate as to enemy peoples—the Ute-Paiute and/or the Apache
(including the original ancestral Navaho)—or drought and arroyo-cutting,
or both, still continues, and will be omitted here.

In any case, we now can state with a reasonable degree of assurance
the connections between most of the living tribes of Southwestern Indians,
other than Athapaskans and Ute-Paiute, and late-prehistoric archeological
groups.

In the period known as Pueblo IV, or Fusion period, from about
1300 A.D. to the Pueblo Revolt and Reconquest (1680 to 1706), the
present distribution of sedentary Southwestern Indians was taking form.
Immediately before the fourteenth century, quite a different arrangement
is visible in the archeological remains. At, let us say, 1250 A.D. there
were several well-known, large, and important groups which later disappeared entirely as such or moved completely out of their then homes—
Mimbres, Tularosa, Mesa Verde, Gallina, and others further west. What
became of some of these people (e.g., the Mimbres group) is completely
unknown. Certain specific continuities, however, can be traced.

The best-known Southwestern cultural group is that of the San Juan
Anasazi found before 1300 in the area north of the Little Colorado, characterized by gray pottery, full-grooved stone axes, circular kivas, and lambdoid deformation. Puebloan occupation of the San Juan apparently ceased
abruptly, while Anasazi traits largely survived in the continuing and
greatly increasing population of the upper Rio Grande.

In particular, black-on-white pottery of Mesa Verde type appeared
suddenly in the Galisteo Basin, just south of Santa Fe, about 1300 when
the Anasazi of the Mesa Verde phase (1150 to 1300) were abandoning
the upper San Juan area. As I have suggested previously, it appears very
reasonable to assume that the Tanoan languages of the upper Rio Grande
may be generally connected with the Anasazi archeological remains of that
area and of the upper San Juan (Chaco Canyon, Mesa Verde, etc.) and,
specifically, that the original inhabitants of the upper Rio Grande (the
sparse pre-1300 population) were speakers of the archaic and divergent

Tiwa dialects. Possibly the Mesa Verde-Galisteo people were Tewa-speaking; they were evidently the ancestors of the modern "Hano" (Tano; the Tewa village on First Mesa in the Hopi country, whither the majority of the Tanos moved from the Santa Cruz valley in 1696 to 1706).

The other Tewa pueblos, north of Santa Fe and mostly still there, must also derive from a San Juan Anasazi source, probably by infiltration or small-scale immigration rather than invasion. I cannot explain satisfactorily the Towa (Jemez-Pecos) language, the disappearance of the Gallina complex (unless it and Towa can be tied together), or the Keresans (who will be discussed further below).

To the west, in what is now northeastern Arizona, the westernmost Mesa Verde people (in the Canyon de Chelly area) and the rather different western San Juan Anasazi of the Kayenta branch (in the Tsegi and the Wupatki area) must have moved in to the Hopi country. Several major elements of post-1300 Hopi Culture are Little Colorado rather than Anasazi; but it is generally felt that the Hopi language (related to Paviotso and Ute-Paiute) was probably that of the Kayenta Anasazi.

In the Zuni country also, a combination of several distinct elements is indicated: (1) a comparatively sparse occupation before 1275 or 1300, of San Juan Anasazi type (black-on-white pottery, circular kivas, lambdoid cranial deformation); (2) a great increase of population and concentration in large centers, with glaze-paint redware, square kivas, 3/4-grooved axes, extended inhumation of the dead, which obviously represents a spread of the Cibola development of the White Mountains region (southeastern Little Colorado and upper Salt River drainage); (3) appearance of considerable Gila Polychrome pottery and the practice of cremation, both from southern Arizona, presumably between 1400 and 1500 (cremation was in use when the Spaniards arrived in 1540). It is probable, I suppose, that the Zuni language (distantly related to Tanoan and, more remotely, to Hopi) belongs with the second and major group, though it is not possible to defend this assumption in detail.

We still have the Keresan-speaking group to account for (Acoma, and five pueblos above the confluence of the Rio Grande and the Jemez River). The language is completely unrelated to the other Pueblo tongues (all of which, together with Piman, are Azteco-Tanoan, or at least—in a conservative view—Uto-Aztecan and Tanoan; and possibly, therefore, "Macro-Penutian"; while Keresan is Hokan-Siouan if anything, and consequently may be related to Yuman).

In previous papers, I have pointed out that the great division within the general Puebloan group, between Anasazi (northern) and Mogollon (southern brownware), corresponds in a rough way to that between the ethnographic Western Pueblos (Hopi, Zuni, Acoma) and Eastern (Rio Grande) Pueblos, and that elements or influences from the Mogollon tradition penetrated, even dominated, Hopi and Zuni toward 1300 A.D. Among these western features in the Zuni area, though not appearing at Hopi, is glaze-paint redware.

In the Acoma district, an early occupation of San Juan Anasazi type carries up to about 1300 or after with Mesa Verde black-on-white at that time. Glaze-paint redware and rectangular kivas apparently came in only after 1300. Now, in the section of the Rio Grande directly east of Acoma, these same two significant traits were introduced from the west about 1350 or slightly before. The immigrants must have been absorbed completely, unless they were Keresans. Other hypotheses in recent years have correlated Keresan with Mesa Verde, and with the non-Mesa Verde element in Chaco Canyon (and, therefore, with the Wingate area); either one is also possible. Nobody has yet suggested, however, that the Keresans have been in the Rio Grande all along.

In any case, though no single hypothesis has been generally agreed upon, it is possible to "account for" the modern pueblos and to connect most if not all of the archeological groups of the northern Southwest with living peoples. In central and southern New Mexico, it has to be assumed that the Piro Indians (pueblos, extinct as such since 1680, a few descendants still living in the El Paso vicinity; a Tanoan language particularly close to Tiwa) were descendants of the local and nearby pre-Spanish people whose archeology, not well-known, is more of southern (Mogollon) than Anasazi affiliation. The Mimbres and Chihuahua groups, however, simply disappear from the record.

To the west, the Yuman tribes (non-puebloan, semi-sedentary horticultural) of western Arizona can be derived with assurance from the Patayan archeological groups. In southern Arizona, the connection between archeological remains of mixed Hohokam and Mogollon type and Piman-speaking tribes has begun to receive confirmation through DiPeso's work already mentioned.

Finally, it is another source for gratification that archeologists no longer feel impelled to stop at A.D. 1540, 1600, or 1700, or to ignore or deprecate the doings of the European invaders and the effects of Spanish Catholic civilization upon the indigenous peoples, as is so clearly shown by the following work: Brew's 1935-39 work at Awatovi, including the Franciscan Mission; Toulouse's (1949) report on Abó Mission; DiPeso's (1953) study of the Spanish remains at Quiburi; Ellis' (1953) consideration of European influence on Pueblo pottery; Wendorf's (1953) recent excavations at

57

Cuyamunge; and an increasing arousal of interest in acculturation and in process (rather than sheer chronicle) generally.

There still remain many large questions wide open, as well as comparatively minor arguments as to which group of Anasazi entering the Rio Grande spoke which Tanoan dialect, or as to which type of black-on-red pottery was made first in what area by whom. A few of these are: when and by what route or routes did the Apache come into the Southwest and, inevitably connected with that one, were the San Juan Anasazi and several other puebloan groups forced out of their original home-lands by the pressure of an enemy people? These first two queries will be at least partly answered by findings in connection with the Navaho land claims investigations; but another one will remain—where were the ancestors of the Utes, and what were they doing before about 1750? Turning southward and to an earlier period, were the true Hohokam, with the highly distinctive culture of the Colonial and Sedentary periods, a Mexican group abruptly invading southern Arizona? If so, are the "Pioneer Hohokam" preceding them to be considered Yuman-Patayan, Mogollon, or what? Can the prehistoric Cohonina and Prescott branches, with Patayan ceramics but several puebloan traits, be connected somehow with the upland Yumans, or did they simply disappear? What became of the puebloan or puebloid occupants of southwestern Utah, and the Moapa Valley of southern Nevada and why did these complexes disappear toward, apparently, 1150 A.D.? Why did the population of Chaco Canyon decline markedly between about 1130 and the 1200's? What happened to the Mimbres people during the same period? Where did the Keresan-speakers come from? Getting back to more fundamental matters, from exactly what outside sources, and just how, did the peoples of the Southwest originally receive pottery-making, the bow and arrow, pit houses, and various other traits; and to what degree and by what routes were outside contacts kept up through later centuries?

Fortunately for those interested in this area, there are still plenty of specific unsolved problems to attack, and unsettled questions to debate; Southwestern archeology will have unfinished business on hand for a long time yet.

SOURCES OF NORTHWEST COAST CULTURE

Philip Drucker

TO BRING together the materials on Northwest Coast culture and to attempt to coordinate those data into historically meaningful formulations is both easy and perilous: easy because there is a wealth of ethnographic informa- tion available plus a few linguistic and anthropometric data, and only a modicum of cold, hard, archeologic fact to refute one's interpretations. By the same token it is perilous for one is tempted to rely far too heavily on ethnographic distributions in which subjective evaluations must be made as to which culture traits are and which are not similar and, further, arbitrary assumptions must be made as to the significance of those distribu- tions especially of the discontinuous ones. For example, was the Southern Kwakiutl custom of storing salmon heads in pits technologically and his- torically (not to say gustatorially) related to the "pit-ripening" of olachen?[1] Can this trait be regarded as identical with the more northerly pit-storage of salmon roe for the tracing of distributions? If so, do breaks in the dis- tribution mean the pit-storage trait in some form was once universal in the north and later discarded by people like the Coast Tsimshian and Haisla? When relying so heavily on materials of this sort without the controls defined by archeological sequences and relationships, there is but a thin dividing line between the posing of a bold but methodologically valid hypothesis and the unfortunate tactic of rushing out on a limb and sawing it off behind one. If I accomplish the latter rather than the former, it is not without being aware of the danger.

THE PROBLEM

It has been recognized for a long time that the Northwest Coast occupies an anomalous position in the broad overall pattern of native American civilizations. First of all, it is an area of advanced cultures with

---

[1] This is the famous "candlefish" (Thaleichthys pacificus).

highly elaborate technologies and intricate social and ceremonial systems based upon a wild food subsistence economy, forming an exception to the general rule that only simpler, more "primitive" cultures are associated with such an economic base. Again, the real culture patterns appear to have had slight connections, if any, with those of the advanced civilizations of Middle America from which most other comparatively advanced North American cultures can be derived.

PREVIOUS HYPOTHESES

The older interpretation of Northwest Coast culture origins formulated by Boas, which guided the work of the famous Jesup Expedition, stressed the similarities to aboriginal cultures of northeast Asia. That is to say, Northwest Coast culture was seen as a result of a flow of cultural influences from Asia to North America along the North Pacific littoral. This was believed to have resulted in a continued transplanting of essentially non-American cultural traditions, interrupted only by "the intrusion of the Eskimo into the Bering Sea Area" (Boas, 1905, 1933). This whole interpretation was closely related, of course, to Boas' *idée fixe* regarding the Central Canadian Arctic origin of the Eskimo. Now there can be little doubt that a considerable number of culture traits were diffused between northeast Asia and northwest America both across the Bering Sea and along the Aleutian chain. The findings of the Jesup Expedition stressed certain of these: slat and plate armor, the compound bow, the tambourine drum, the Raven myth cycle. More recent work has shown that this list can be expanded considerably[2] and that, in addition, there is evidence of transmissions not only from Asia to America but also from America to Asia. However, it obviously makes a great deal of difference in appraising cultural relationships and reconstructing culture history if the Eskimo-Aleut did not disrupt a stream of diffusion but participated in it, actually forming an integral link in the transmission of traits and complexes between continents. With modern information on Eskimo origins, based upon solid archeological fact, Boas' theory becomes untenable. The Old Bering Sea date of about 250 B.C. and one of about 1000 B.C. for an early Aleutian horizon change the whole picture. Present evidence indicates that the shores of Bering Sea formed a focus of development, elaboration, and divergence of the varied

---

[2] Heizer (1943, pp. 452-453) summarizes comparative analyses made by Collins, de Laguna, and Birket-Smith and de Laguna. Heizer's paper is itself a convincing demonstration of the diffusion of a complex from northeast Asia across the Aleutians as far eastward as Kodiak and the Alaska Peninsula.

Eskimo and Aleut cultures in the course of their growth from the Old World Mesolithic pattern exemplified by the Cape Denbigh materials dated at about 6000 years ago. Hence, any northeast Asiatic concepts, whether of major or minor significance in Northwest Coast culture growth, must have been transmitted to the Northwest Coast peoples by Eskimo-Aleut.

Kroeber (1923) offered a different interpretation of Northwest Coast culture some years ago. According to this view, the civilization of the area was a highly specialized but essentially American Indian culture. Kroeber considered that it might have come into being as interior groups worked their way downstream along the various major rivers that empty into the Pacific, becoming first riparian and eventually maritime as they reached salt water. In the process, the distinctive patterns of areal culture, he believed, were developed. There are a number of seemingly valid objections to this hypothesis. One of the most impressive is that none of the distinctive major motifs of Northwest Coast culture can be derived from concepts prevalent in the cultures of the adjacent interior. Consider, if you will, the corollary of validation through distribution of valuables (the so-called "potlatch"). Nowhere in the whole New World was there less interest in fixed rank and material wealth than in the bordering interior, from the Yukon-Mackenzie drainages through Plateau, Great Basin, and the Southwest, except where Northwest Coast influences had created duplications of Coastal patterns, as among some Athabascan neighbors of the Tlingit, and in north central California. Even the simplest component of the complex, an interest in wealth comprised of surplus goods, does not reappear until we reach the Eastern Woodlands and Southeast, and the late High Plains patterns derived from the eastward. Therefore, to attempt to derive basic Northwest Coast patterns from the interior, that is, from the culture or cultures found on or near the headwaters of major drainage systems that cut through to the coast, means we must assume that tremendous changes in cultural orientation have occurred throughout the whole interior which transformed the patterns that contained the seeds of Northwest Coast motifs into the rather colorless, close-to-bare-subsistence patterns known from the ethnographic horizon.

A second objection to Kroeber's interpretation involves a subjective appraisal but seems to have some validity. While one may conceive of interior groups emerging and gradually adapting to the coast in the southern half of the area, it is difficult to see how this could be done in the north with its abrupt transition from interior to coastal environments, its precipitous rocky coasts, huge tides, and its fauna abundant but difficult of access. In other words, it would seem that the first human inhabitants of the northern coasts could not have coped with the environment had they not already been competent seamen with some skill at the techniques of deepsea fishing and hunting. If the coast was first populated in the fashion pictured by Kroeber, then it would have to be in the south that the interior people worked their way downstream to gradually become maritime, thereafter pushing northward. If such had been the case, we should expect the cultural climax to occur in the southern part of the area, with a decrease in cultural complexity and intensity toward the north. This is obviously not the case. There was a subclimax in northwest California but it was far behind the northern centers in its integration and accentuation of areal patterns. The Lower Columbia was a market place through which vast quantities of Northwest Coast material goods passed in trade but it contributed little in cultural elaboration. Puget Sound was culturally speaking a cul-de-sac, an internal "marginal" region from the areal point of view. In brief, while there are numbers of interior culture traits to be found along the several parts of the coast, neither the basic distinctive patterns of the area nor the typical way of life can be explained as a simple infiltration of interior tribes down the river valleys.

There is another theoretically possible source of cultural influence which must be considered in connection with the Northwest Coast: Direct trans-Pacific contact. There are enough documented instances of east Asiatic (apparently mostly Japanese?) hulks that the Japanese Current washed aground on Northwest Coast beaches to make it clear that material objects from East Asia must have become available to the Indians, and numbers of contacts with survivors aboard some of the wrecks certainly occurred over the centuries.[3] However, the Pacific regions in which the most numerous cultural resemblances to Northwest Coast patterns occur—Melanesia and parts of Indonesia—are so remote as to make it highly unlikely that materials, much less people, could ever drift to the coasts of North America. Kroeber has discussed these Northwest Coast-Oceanic similarities,[4] and has made it clear that not only are tremendous distances involved, but, in addition "the similarities are not in specific traits, but in broad features building

---

[3] The problem of the possible influence of Asiatic personnel who reached the American coasts aboard wrecked junks has been disposed of by Kroeber (1948a, p. 561) ". . . there is historical record of Oriental and European vessels being wrecked on the Pacific coast of North America, during the last century and a half, among tribes that were still almost wholly aboriginal. In no case did the natives make a serious attempt to absorb the higher culture of the strangers. Generally these were enslaved or killed, their property rifled; sometimes the wreck was set on fire."

[4] He lists "social status dependent on wealth; accurate systems of valuing shell money or treasures; large-scale distributions of food and property at competitive gift festivals or potlatches; membership in secret societies serving as a prestige symbol of rank; use of masks in the rituals of such societies; and elaborate wood-carving."

into a connected pattern of cultural slant. They may thus well be the result of fortuitously converging generic trends. . ." (1948a, p. 783).

Even if some specific traits could be found that might suggest genetic relationship of the patterns, it seems far more likely to the present writer that the Indonesian-Melanesian and the Northwest Coast patterns represent the end products of two separate cultural currents flowing out of east Asia. There are some very curious parallels between Northwest Coast and east Asiatic elements of culture in addition to the generic Oceanic similarities just mentioned. Some of these, particularly those relating to northeast Asia, have been stressed in discussions of the results of the Jesup Expeditions (Boas, 1905 and 1933). Others are very peculiarly distributed both in time and space. Perhaps the most striking and least explicable are two stylistic concepts found in Shang and Early Chou art on the one hand and northern Northwest Coast art on the other: The use of stylized animal forms drawn or modeled as though they were split down the back with the two sides spread symmetrically on either side of the front-view head; and the use of rectangular elements with rounded corners often referred to as "eye" elements in discussions of Northwest Coast art (and similar as well to the oval "eye" elements of Old Bering Sea art; Collins, 1937, p. 298). Until archeological work has traced out the developmental phases of the American Indian art, it is useless to speculate on relationships of the two styles. The Pacific littoral distribution of rod- or slat-armor is well known; however, the very striking similarity of the northern, especially Tlingit, helmet-visor-armor combination to East Asiatic defensive equipment has not been sufficiently stressed. In fine, while trans-Pacific contacts undoubtedly occurred many times they were probably inconsequential as regards culture influence, and the generic Oceanic cultural similarities must be viewed either as accidental convergences or as the results of cultural influences from the Asiatic mainland which simultaneously affected two widely sep-arated geographic areas.

NEW HYPOTHESIS

So far, I have pointed out what appear to be critical deficiencies in a variety of hypotheses as to Northwest Coast culture origins: The trans-planted Northeast Asiatic culture theory of Boas; the theory of indigenous origin held by Kroeber; and the direct trans-Pacific importation possibility. My purpose in so doing was to bring out certain significant qualities of Northwest Coast culture, and certain factors which must have affected

63

its historical development. These qualities and factors can be translated into positive terms as follows:

1. Northwest Coast culture was fundamentally distinct from all other Indian cultures of western North America.

2. There is no indication that the trans-Pacific contacts, either from east Asia or Oceania, that may have occurred, had any important effects on areal culture growth.

3. There are evidences of northwest Asiatic and possibly east Asiatic influences, in the form of some specific traits and perhaps some culture complexes, which may have been components of a flow of cultural influence extending over a long period of time.

4. These Asiatic influences could not have been transmitted prior to the development of Eskimo-Aleut Culture in southwest Alaska and the Bering Sea region, but must have been transmitted by Eskimo-Aleut.

5. The Coast, at least in its northern part, must have been first occupied by a people who entered it already equipped to live a maritime life, not by Indians fresh out of the interior.

In formulating a hypothesis which will be consistent with all the above, item 4 offers our best lead. If the various Asiatic elements were transmitted to the Northwest Coast by Eskimo and/or Aleut, a much closer and older connection than has heretofore been considered likely between Northwest Coast and Eskimo-Aleut cultures must have existed. If such an enduring and intimate cultural relationship existed, might not an early maritime sea-hunting and fishing form of Eskimo-Aleut culture have provided the basic patterns from which Northwest Coast culture as we know it from the ethnographic horizon may have developed? This thought may be put in the form of a hypothesis. *Proposed: that the distinctive basic patterns of the Northwest Coast culture, from Yakutat Bay to northwest California, were derived from the same subarctic fishing-and-sea-hunting base of the coasts of Bering Sea and southwest Alaska that gave rise to the various Eskimo and Aleut cultures.*[5]

---

[5] This proposition, in the broad form presented here, is new. What we might call constituent parts of it, referring to possible cultural affiliations of certain Northwest Coast groups to Eskimo-Aleut cultures, are not. The present writer has suggested such linkages in previous studies and both Borden (1951) and Lantis (1938) have done the same, with particular reference to the Nootka and Nootka whaling. Collins (1937, 1940) called attention to a number of significant Esk no-Northwest Coast parallels some time ago. De Laguna (1947) has also stressed the importance of Eskimo-Northwest Coast cultural relationships, though regarding them as much more recent phenomena than the present writer. Kroeber, qualifying his earlier position, has remarked, "It is, of course, possible that at an earlier period, when the Northwest Coast culture was as yet less developed, the Eskimo influence was the more potent, but that the elements derived from it have long since been worked over so as to seem native Northwestern" (1939, p. 29). Thus, though retaining his view as to the indigenous development of Northwest Coast culture, Kroeber suggests the possibility of an old and more intimate connection between that tradition and that of the Eskimo.

64

The testing of this postulate must be by cultural evidence, not racial or linguistic. What with the highly complex situation in the physical anthropology of the Eskimo-Aleut in the region south of the Kuskokwim and the paucity of data in the same field on the Northwest Coast, it is still impossible to identify Eskimo-Aleut somatologic elements among the Coast Indians or to demonstrate their absence. Linguistically, there is no known evidence of any relationship between Eskimo-Aleut and any Northwest Coast Indian tongue.

ETHNOGRAPHIC EVIDENCE

Subdivisions and Climax of Northwest Coast Culture

In terms of both coverage and sheer volume, the ethnographic materials comprise the best body of data on the cultures of the area. Ethnographic data may be utilized in two ways in a study of historic nature. First, the interrelationships of a group or groups of individual cultures may be appraised, and second, longer range comparisons involving continuous or discontinuous traits or complexes may be made. I am 'assuming here that the salient features that distinguish Northwest Coast ethnography as a whole are familiar enough to the reader so that a summary list of them will serve to define the areal patterns. From Yakutat Bay (Fig. 4) in the Gulf of Alaska to Trinidad Bay in northern California, native cultures included the following distinctive features: Economies built around fishing with elaborate series of types of fish traps, harpoons, and angling devices; sea mammal hunting both as a food source and even more for prestige; relatively slight use of vegetable foods; emphasis on wood working; rectangular plank houses; specialized varieties of dugout canoes and emphasis on water transportation; untailored (wrap-around or slip over) garments principally of plant fibers; barefootedness; lineage-local group as the basic social unit; hereditary rank-wealth correlation defining status and emphasis on status in social affairs; slavery; elaboration of ceremonialism (potlatch, dancing societies, wealth displays); and "First Salmon" rites and related types of ceremonies derived from belief in the immortality of game species. These were the features that united the cultures of the Northwest Coast into a distinctive areal pattern as weft strands tie in a series of warps into a single whole.

It is nonetheless obvious even from the most superficial survey that the individual cultures of the Northwest Coast were not all exactly alike. Over-

65

lying the basic areal patterns summarized above was a series of local differ-ences and specializations. These patterns of limited distributions may be utilized to distinguish subunits or what we may refer to as "provinces" within the area. This cultural variation indicates, of course, differing regional histories which must be taken into account in the interpretation of areal cultural growth. Comparative distributions suggest four of these provinces (Fig. 4) whose boundaries are fairly sharp.[6] From north to south these are: (1) The Northern Province, which included the Tlingit, Haida, Tsimshian, and Haisla; (2) the Wakashan Province, which included all Kwakiutl (other than the Haisla), the Nootka, and in addition the Bella Coola; (3) the Coast Salish-Chinook Province, which included the groups speaking those languages from the Gulf of Georgia to the central Oregon coast, and which contained as well a series of small enclaves of diverse linguistic affiliations (Chemakum, Quileute, Athabascan); and (4) the Northwest California Province, whose center lay among the Yurok, Karok, and Hupa of the Lower Klamath River and included also the culturally marginal Athabascan and Wiyot neighbors of these groups. Table I lists in summary fashion the outstanding distinctive features of each of these four provinces. In Table 2, some cultural features common to two or three of these divisions are presented to indicate interprovincial relationship (pp. 79-81).

The main contribution of linguistics to our attempt to reconstruct areal culture history is that the native languages spoken fall into blocks which correspond closely with the cultural divisions just outlined. In addi-tion, many linguists believe that certain languages have fairly close interior affiliations, such as those between Haida, Tlingit, and Athabascan (and Eyak). The kinship of Coast and Interior Salish has never, to my knowl-edge, been questioned by linguists. Just how the lexico-statistical studies made by Swadesh (1950, 1952a, 1952b) tie together cannot be appraised as yet, but if his temporal conclusions have any validity at all they point toward a length of occupation of the coast comparable to that of southwest Alaska.

Practically nothing except a limited amount of blood-typing has been done in physical anthropology on the Northwest Coast since Boas took measurements there in the past century (Boas, 1895). His results indicate a distribution of physical types that corresponds pretty well to the cultural divisions outlined in preceding paragraphs: The groups of the Northern Province form a fairly sharply defined unit, distinct from those of the Wakashan Province; the Coast Salish (except the Bella Coola, who con-form to the Wakashan type as they did in most respects in provincial cul-

---

[6] This classification is presented here for the first time. It differs somewhat from that of Kroeber (1939, pp. 28ff).

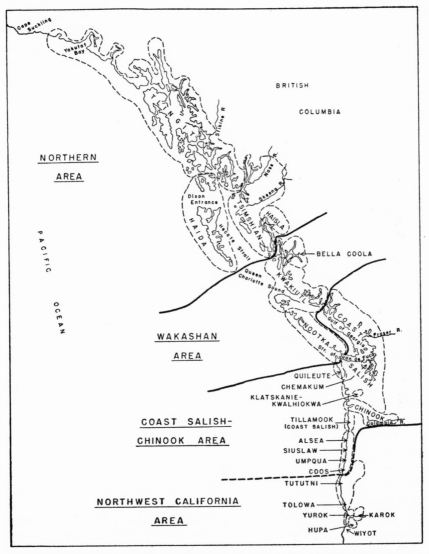

Fig. 4.—Culture Areas and Tribal Distributions of the Northwest Coast.

ture pattern), represent a third type which, incidentally, differs but little from that of their Interior Salish kinsmen. The chief difference from the cultural grouping occurs on the lower Columbia: It appears that the Chinook differed more physically than they did culturally from their Salish neighbors. The Northwest Californians are set apart physically as well as culturally: It would seem that they belong definitely to native California.

If we sketch the extra-areal relationships of these individual provinces, we find what may at first glance seem to be a common-place fact but one which has some interesting implications. That is to say, each of the provinces save one shows evidence of considerable contact with neighboring cultures of the interior. In the Northern Province, such items as sinew-backed bows, bows with string-guard, men's breechcloth, leggings, occasional use of porcupine-quill embroidery, Athabascan-type snowshoes, cremation of the dead, and possibly matrilineal organization, all point to cultural influence from the Athabascan peoples of the interior. Certain Tlingit groups like the Chilkat departed from usual coastal custom by wearing tailored buckskin garments cut precisely like those of neighbors in the hinterland. The Tsimshian-speaking Niska and Gitksan wore similar apparel in the wintertime. We know, of course, that these groups carried on extensive trade with the interior, a commerce which was intensified during the earlier fur trade period.

Further south in the Coast Salish-Chinook Province, we find another set of distinctive interior traits. These, however, are specifically Plateau-Great Basin elements and include mat lodges (as temporary dwellings), coiled basketry, truncated conical basketry caps for women, small steam sweat lodge, use of long nets for fishing and hunting. One of the two textile-weaving patterns in this Province, that of the twilled, checker, dog hair (or dog hair and mountain goat wool) blanket, although woven on an elaborate double bar loom, was technologically very close to and probably derived from the woven rabbit skin robe of the Plateau and Great Basin. The relatively loosely defined system of social rank in this Province represents either interior influence or a cultural heritage of these people from their interior-dwelling ancestors. The Northwest California Province is distinguished in part by a series of elements which suggest influences from Central California, among them: Women's basketry cap, grinding and leaching of acorns, deer-head decoy, feather-work decoration, and direct fire sweat-bathing.

It is only the Wakashan Province in which no specifically interior cultural traits can be identified, suggesting that the speakers of the Wakashan languages may have been isolated from interior influences for a very long time.[7] In a certain sense, then, the Wakashan-speakers may be regarded as the *most typical coastal peoples of all*, since their culture lacks interior influences.

This appraisal can be reinforced in another way. Although it has been a habit among anthropologists to regard the Northern Province as representing the areal climax, in terms of complexity and elaboration of areal themes, there are actually few aspects of culture in which it surpassed the Wakashan division. The spectacular "totem pole" art, the so-called Chilkat blanket, and the complex clan-crest system are usually referred to among the outstanding achivements of the north. However, although the Wakashan people adopted the totem pole only in recent historic times, their principal and more important older carvings, especially in their masks, houseposts, feast dishes, and the like, incorporate a vigor of concept and a sense of movement that by most esthetic standards surpasses the rigidly stylized, somewhat static totem pole art. The Chilkat blanket appears to have been but one of a series of technically related textile products woven as far south as the Straits of Juan de Fuca in Coast Salish territory. Crests, to the Wakashan-speakers, were but one variety of a host of hereditary "privileges." Among the achievements of these same Wakashan-speakers (practiced by some or all of them), we find: Maximum elaboration of graded social statuses; elaboration of the dramatic rituals of the Dancing Societies (or "secret societies," as they have been called), greatest emphasis on sea-hunting, including whaling, and sea-hunting ritual; maximum development of potlatching. The Nootkans presumably invented the mechanically ingenious dentalia-picking apparatus; most of the groups of the northern coasts agree in ascribing the invention of the equally ingenious funnel-shaped olachen net to the Kwakiutl. In other words, in terms of complexity of pattern and of achieving the greatest degree of elaboration of areal themes, the groups of the Wakashan Province stand out. They should, therefore, be regarded as "most typical" and as forming the principal focal center of the Northwest Coast area.

---

[7] The Bella Coola, while forming a part of this province on the ethnographic-time horizon, are excluded from consideration here as presumably being a special case. It is worth noting that, while they have taken over practically all the technological and ceremonial patterns of their Kwakiutl neighbors, they deviate sharply from provincial patterns in one point: They seem to have retained the same loose and flexible system of social rank as that which distinguished their Salish kinsmen and former neighbors to the south and east.

Eskimo-Aleut and Northwest Coast cultural parallels[8] fall into several categories, which will be treated in turn:

(a) Traits common to all or most Eskimo-Aleut and to all or most Northwest Coast provinces;

(b) Traits found principally among Eskimo of the Bering Sea-Southwest Alaska regions, the Aleut, and all or most Northwest Coast provinces;

(c) Traits found among some or all Eskimo-Aleut and in one or at most two Northwest Coast provinces.

In Category (a), we find such basic features as the whole fishing-and-sea-hunting orientation of both Eskimo-Aleut and Northwest Coast cultures. High development of marine transport was part and parcel of this economic bias. It is true that most Eskimo stressed sea-hunting more than fishing, but that was probably due to the restricted distribution of salmon in their territory; where salmon ran in the rivers they utilized them considerably. This emphasis on the maritime-slanted economy is not simply a matter of local geography. The Indians who created the San Francisco Bay shell mounds certainly depended heavily upon fish and products of the foreshore but their culture remained intrinsically Central Californian. Significant throughout the length of the Northwest Coast was the vast prestige set on sea hunting, even though it was not as economically rewarding as fishing. Witness, for example, the northwestern Californians, who quite literally took their lives in their hands when they put to sea in their narrow-waisted, cranky, river canoes. With the woods full of deer, they set out on sea-lion hunts for the glory to be attained thereby.

A second pattern fundamental to both cultures was a highly developed craftsmanship particularly associated with woodworking. That woodworking was an outstanding feature of Northwest Coast culture is so familiar as to be trite; that Eskimo and Aleut were also masters of the craft is sometimes overlooked, perhaps because these people also utilized bone, horn, and ivory extensively. These last-named materials were handled with woodworking techniques, however, and in certain instances were used as substitutes for wood.

---

[8] I have not made a minute inventory of Eskimo cultures, but have selected the better known and most obvious parallels; my list can unquestionably be supplemented.

As Collins (1937, p. 284) pointed out some years ago, the square or rectangular wooden house is both the oldest and the most nearly universal Eskimo type (with the exception of Dorset). The occurrence of the same rectangular plank house down the Northwest Coast forms a single con- tinuous distribution with the old Eskimo type. All other house types on the Northwest Coast are so aberrant that they have invariably been inter- preted as representing interior heritages or influence.

Toggling harpoon heads are, of course, both ancient and universal among Eskimo cultures. They recur in slightly variant form—composite rather than one piece—in all the Northwest Coast provinces save the Northern one and, in fact, spilled over into native California. The detach- able barbed points of the Northern Province (sometimes referred to as toggle-heads but technically quite distinct) were also used by Eskimo and Aleut but since they belong to an old (European Paleolithic) and nearly world-wide type are probably not significant in connection with the present problem.

A very fundamental religious concept of the Northwest Coast, and one which is also basic to a major part of Eskimo-Aleut ceremonialism, is the belief in the immortality of game. Along with this belief there is the ritual requirement of honoring captured animals and of returning certain parts (bones, offal, bladders, etc.) to the sea. The Western Eskimo and Aleut elaborated rituals about this theme principally in connection with sea mammals; the Indians applied it principally to fish, in their "First Salmon" rites, but there are extensions to other species such as whales, bear, moun- tain goat, and the like.

Belief in soul-loss as a major cause of disease seems to be basic to Eskimo shamanism. It was also prominent in Northwest Coast except in the heart of the Northwest California Province. Although the Puget Sound Salish "spirit canoe ceremony" seems most spectacular, the Nootka dupli- cated Eskimo usage and concept most closely: The shaman, made fast to a long line, went himself from the house down into the sea to recover the errant or stolen soul, then was hauled back by his aids who heaved in the line to which he was tied. This "shaman's journey under the sea" is a fairly common variant of another Eskimo theme, "the shaman's journey to the moon."

Traits of Category (b), those limited to Bering Sea and Pacific Eskimo and Aleut, but widespread on the Northwest Coast, include some which are probably ancient in Eskimo culture, but which were discarded as impractical or impossible by the Thule people who moved eastward along the inhos- pitable Arctic shores. Other elements may be those which filtered through from Northeast Asia after the initial eastward Thule movement. These items

71

include: wooden dishes and food trays; wooden boxes with bent sides and fitted lids; twined basketry; habitual barefootedness; use of urine as detergent, with ritualistic connotations; slat and plate armor; head-taking in war; mourning ceremonials; property distribution ("potlatches") at ceremonials; grave monuments. Some of these concepts and complexes among Eskimo have been brushed aside as representing "diffusion from the Northwest Coast" due to preconceived notions as to what constituted "typical Northwest Coast culture." There is not, however, the least evidence to indicate that the direction of diffusion was necessarily from Indians to Eskimo-Aleut. On the contrary (partly, it is true, because there are more Eskimo archeologic data), there is older evidence of various of these features from Eskimo cultures. An elaborate ceremonialism of respectable antiquity is certainly indicated by the Ipiutak materials; the ivory masks and the carvings of skulls hint at mourning or commemorative rites. Whether potlatches accompanied these rites is, naturally, something that archeology cannot reveal.

The general effect of the foregoing distributions is to suggest that a close and fundamental relationship between Eskimo-Aleut and Northwest Coast culture continued to be effective over a long period of time.

Traits of Category (c), which includes those of both universal and of restricted distribution among Eskimo-Aleut and of only limited distribution on the Coast, are particularly revealing for they clearly suggest differing degrees of intensity and probably antiquity of affiliation of segments of the two cultures.

With the Northern Province, Eskimo-Aleut cultures share a number of items of material culture: heavy splitting adzes; hafted stone mauls (also Northern Kwakiutl); the tambourine drum; wooden h ts;[9] bone needle cases; umiaks (Northern Tlingit only on the Coast); and the well-known Cross Sound throwing boards collected by Vancouver (Dalton, 1897, pl. 15; Read, 1891, fig. 3). It will be noted that, with the exception of the wooden hats, all these are objects that could have been acquired, or whose prototype could have been acquired, in trade or as booty of war. They are objects whose utility is rather obvious; they appear to be the sort of materials that could be transferred across linguistic and cultural boundaries with but the most casual sort of contact.

If we turn now to Eskimo-Aleut traits and complexes recurring in the Wakashan Province, we will find a series of features of quite different order. Of these, one of the most spectacular is the hunting of whales. Lantis (1938) and Borden (1951) have both called attention to the similarity

---

[9] Here there is an arbitrary categorization: the bent wooden hats of the Aleut and Koniag may not be closely related to the carved, one-piece wooden hats (not helmets) of the Tlingit.

of the Nootka and Eskimo whaling. Their comparison, however, requires re-definition. One difficulty in the past has been the fact that Nootka whaling described in the earlier sources appeared most similar to Eskimo whaling in gear and technique, but Nootkan ritual procedure reportedly associated with the complex was most similar to the rites of Aleut and Koniag. In actuality, the Nootka had two different types of whaling which they differentiated sharply. One, in which harpoons and the floats were used from a big canoe, was associated with ritual procedures similar to those of the Eskimo of Bering Strait and the Arctic Coast, in which there were only minimum associations with the dead. The other kind of Nootka "whaler" did not actually hunt at sea but was a ritualist who mobilized the supernatural powers of the dead to cause dead whales to drift ashore. He was the "whaler" who constructed the elaborate shrines filled with corpses so much like the shrines of the Aleut whalers. If both Nootka whaling patterns have any genetic relationship with those of the Eskimo and the Aleut, as seems highly probable, then both complexes must have been acquired after the differentiation of Eskimo and Aleut cultures with their distinctive whaling complexes. Eskimo harpoon-and-float whaling may have occurred in Old Bering Sea times but apparently reached its full development only in the Punuk period, whose beginning is placed at about the end of the first millennium A.D. There is no certain evidence as yet as to the date of the beginning of the Aleut-Koniag complex though Heizer suggests it may be more recent than the harpoon-and-float technique (Heizer, 1943, pp. 447ff).

Even if one wishes to take the extreme view that the Nootka-Eskimo and Nootka-Aleut whaling complexes are fortuitous parallels, the underlying traits and concepts are certainly related. Not only are there significant similarities between the types of gear used in the harpoon-and-float complexes, but the fundamental ritualistic concept—that the dead exerted power over marine game—was common to these groups, and these alone, in Northwest America.

The fact that the Kwakiutl are not known to have hunted whales raises certain problems. Borden (1951, p. 44) has attempted to separate the arrival time of the Nootka and Kwakiutl on the coast on the basis of this ethnographic difference. This does not seem to follow logically because of the numerous similarities in all other aspects of culture. Consideration must be given to the possibility of the Kwakiutl having once practiced the art, then having abandoned it. To make a guess, it might be that development of the olachen fishing techniques by the ancestral Kwakiutl contributed to loss of interest in whaling. The olachen are certainly a surer and probably more productive source of oil than the more spectacular whales. One fact that supports this conclusion is the Kwakiutl use on their sealing canoes of attached "harpoon rests" which correspond in form and function to the Eskimo umiak harpoon rests.

Boas (1909, p. 495) long ago pointed out the functional similarity of the finger-holes and/or trident finger-rests at the bases of Kwakiutl and Nootka sealing harpoon shafts to the technique of using the throwing board. That this is a significant parallel is suggested by the fact that hurling a harpoon from its base, whether with throwing board or with the hand, involves the development of motor habits very different from those used to hurl the same weapon by the middle of its shaft.

The topic of masks is difficult to handle, because we do not know whether we are dealing with a single trait or with several. Masks were used as disguises on ceremonial occasions by most Western and Pacific Eskimo and sporadically east of the Mackenzie. Just how the strange Ipiutak "masks," if that is what they were, were used is unknown. These objects may have been ritual devices of a different kind. In any case, masks are of wide distribution among Eskimo-Aleut and firmly rooted into the ritual patterns of those people. On the ethnographic horizon, masks were used as disguises in connection with certain rituals on the Northwest Coast south as far as northwestern Washington state. However, their maximum elaboration occurred among the Kwakiutl-Nootka, particularly in connection with the Dancing Society performances. It is probable that Tlingit, Haida, and Tsimshian acquired their masks along with the Dancing Society performances which they adopted from the Kwakiutl, just as those Coast Salish who used masks unquestionably derived them from Nootka and Southern Kwakiutl neighbors. Thus, the making and use of masks must be regarded as another linkage between Eskimo-Aleut and the Wakashan Province rather than with the Northwest Coast in general. The marked typological differences noted by Lantis (1947) between Eskimo-Aleut and Northwest Coast masks may be taken to indicate a period of local differentiation after direct culture contacts ceased.

Another very interesting area of similarity between the Wakashan speakers and Eskimo-Aleut is the emphasis on elaborate mechanical devices, especially for ritualistic purposes. The Eskimo have long been renowned for their ingenious utilization of mechanical principles in their manufactures. Lantis (1947, pp. 51ff., 121) has drawn attention to the significance of string-manipulated objects (puppets, bladders, etc.) in Western Eskimo ceremonialism. Nootka and Kwakiutl elaborated such devices to a tremendous degree for their ceremonies. Figures of monsters and strange beings were made to fly across the house or to appear from and to disappear into the ground while manipulated with lines and other stage equipment. Masks which the wearer operated with concealed strings were made to change their form in the course of a dance. Other coastal tribes eventually acquired some of these devices, particularly in connection with the spread of the Dancing Societies, but their real source and maximum development seems to have been among the Wakashan-speaking groups.

A rather peculiar custom manifested by the Nootka was the conducting of autopsies or dissections of the dead on certain occasions. At times, among the Nootka, when a death appeared to be inexplicable the bereaved relatives would open up the body to attempt to determine the cause of death. The fact that they are said to have found evidences of slaying by magical means far more often than indications of death from natural causes does not detract from the fact that it was a striking practice among a people who ordinarily had so much fear of the dead. Laughlin (1952a, 1952b) has recently emphasized a comparable Aleut practice, and some Eskimos are reported to carry it out as well; Larsen and Rainey (1948, p. 120) present some evidence of its occurrence in their Ipiutak material. In addition, it was an invariable custom for the fetus to be removed for separate burial whenever a pregnant woman died among both the Nootka and a number of Eskimo groups.

Lantis (1947, pp. 27ff). has assembled what bits of information can still be recovered on Eskimo and Aleut secret societies. Specific points of similarity to the Wakashan Dancing Society performances include: masked performers impersonating spirits; performances representing kidnapping, death, and resurrection, including sleight-of-hand representations of cannibalism and other horrendous acts. The reported "grass costumes" of the Aleut and Bering Sea Eskimo cannot fail to remind one of the "sacred cedar bark" insignia of Nootka and Kwakiutl performers, as well as of the wood-shavings used as religious symbols in Northeast Asia. Lantis (loc. cit.) has pointed out the possible association of bullroarers and whistles with the Eskimo-Aleut performances, instruments which were integral elements of the Wakashan complex, of course. If a great part of the Eskimo-Aleut data on their versions of the secret society complex had not been irretrievably lost, we would likely be able to point out a long list of specific parallels.

In the realm of mythology, it is noteworthy that the Dog-Husband theme, associated with group origins, is widespread among Eskimo groups and is also a part of the origin traditions of a number of important Nootka and Kwakiutl family lines.

Eskimo-Aleut cultural parallels with the Coast Salish-Chinook Province alone are scant and inconsequential. The only one that comes to mind is the multiple-point bird dart or spear, a common item among Eskimo hunting kits, found also among Gulf of Georgia Salish. The precise form differs in the two areas, however.

The principal Eskimo-Northwest California Province parallel is the *kashim* complex. In both regions, this involved a special structure, used as men's house, for certain ceremonies and for direct-fire sweatbathing. A special flue was built to the fireplace, which was assigned ritualistic significance and at times served as an exit. However, despite these apparently close resemblances the two occurrences should probably not be regarded as indicative of direct culture contacts. The Northwest California complex probably should be regarded as the northernmost, and perhaps most conservative, extension of the ceremonial house and/or men's house complex that extended through most of native California, and which ultimately derives from the southern Californian ranchería-Southwest ceremonial house-and-bundle complex, which as Strong (1927) demonstrated is genetically akin to the Pueblo kiva (see also Drucker, 1939). I am perfectly willing to bow out of the discussion at this point, leaving it to Southwesterners to explain why their kivas were so very much like the Eskimo *kashim*.

Summary

It appears that the Wakashan-speaking segment of the Northwest Coast represents the purest strain of Coast culture, in the sense of having the least amount of interior influences (always excepting the Bella Coola). Moreover, it is just this province which was the most active culture focus of the area, elaborating and developing areal patterns to their maximum. On the basis of these two conclusions, it can be inferred that the Wakashan Province represents the oldest strain of Northwest Coast civilization. In addition, it is noteworthy that it is precisely this province in which the greatest number of specific Eskimo-Aleut parallels occur. These similarities include a number of abstruse concepts quite different from the rather simple, obvious, Northern Province-Eskimo parallels and indicate the likelihood of sustained culture contacts with early Eskimo-Aleut. Granting these conclusions does not, of course, necessarily *derive* Wakashan culture from an ancestral Eskimo pattern, but it certainly makes the possibility more likely.

ARCHEOLOGICAL EVIDENCE

The archeology of the Northwest Coast has suffered vast neglect in comparison with most other parts of the New World. About the only significant work is that of Borden (1950, 1951) in the Lower Fraser region.

76

Previously, Smith (1907, 1909) found stratigraphic evidence of population change in the same region, but was unable to define any correlated cultural change. Borden, however, has been able to isolate three horizons: (1) A protohistoric and historic stratum typical of the Lower Fraser ethnographic culture; (2) an underlying transitional horizon in which late period elements occur in increasing quantities from bottom to top; and (3) an early horizon with a radiocarbon date of 2430±163 years (Borden, 1954), which was not only far more maritime in orientation than its successors as indicated by emphasis on sea-mammal hunting, but also includes a number of unquestionably Eskimo elements such as one-piece, blade-slotted, toggling harpoon points, harpoon foreshafts of bone, ground slate points and blades (including ulus and examples of the characteristic Eskimo "men's knife"), as well as chipped points, labrets,[10] and realistic figurines. The harpoon toggle-heads differ somewhat from known Eskimo types, which may logically be taken to indicate local specialization. A much more perplexing problem concerns the apparent absence of heavy woodworking tools. Borden suggests this may indicate absence of a heavy woodworking industry, specifically, absence of dugout canoes. This requires the assumption that skin-covered kayaks or similar vessels were used, since reliance on water transport is indicated by quantities of sea-mammal bones in the deposits. Against this interpretation is the fact that woodworking tools, including hafted adzes, occur consistently in such early Eskimo horizons as Early Old Bering Sea ("Okvik"), and in Old Bering Sea proper, as well as in later horizons. Absence of pottery, common to all western Eskimo horizons, is also puzzling. Either Borden's type-station was a camp site, at which an incomplete inventory of tools and weapons was used, or else the culture was only partially of Eskimo origin. We also lack ethnic associations of the early materials. Until a series of skeletal material has been recovered, we can only guess as to whether the early "eskimoid" culture pattern may be referred to the ancestors of the modern Wakashan peoples or not.

SUMMARY AND CONCLUSIONS

Our survey of data on Northwest Coast culture, aimed at testing the hypothesis as to the Eskimo origin of its basic and distinctive patterns, has yielded the following results:

1. Ethnographic materials suggest a breakdown of the area into four cultural subdivisions or provinces, named here, Northern, Wakashan, Coast Salish-Chinook, and Northwest Californian. The

---

[10] Smith found lateral labrets at Eburne (Marpole) midden.

divisions follow major linguistic boundaries fairly well, and are in the main substantiated by available data on physical anthropology, indicating that we are dealing with real populational entities as well as subcultures.

2. There are a number of generic but significant patterns such as maritime orientation, basic house-type, woodworking technology, etc., which appear to be equally universal and fundamental to both Eskimo-Aleut and Northwest Coast culture.

3. In addition to the foregoing, there is a respectably long list of traits and complexes, including both specific and generic items, found in the Wakashan Province, which are either demonstrably widespread or old among Eskimo-Aleut. This is significant because the Wakashan Province boasts both the purest and the most specialized Northwest Coast subculture, and is geographically remote from modern Eskimo territory.

4. The fact that the Eskimo-Aleut parallels of the Northern Province consist chiefly of material objects that could be traded, looted, or copied with a minimum of communication indicates that the contacts of Tlingit, Haida, and Tsimshian with Eskimo-Aleut were not only less close but probably also more recent than those of the Wakashan-speaking groups; in other words, the groups of the Northern Province probably emerged on the coast after the Wakashan-speaking groups, and may actually have disrupted lines of communication of the latter with Eskimo-Aleut.

5. The older interpretation of the relatively late emergence of the Coast Salish remains unchanged.

6. In addition to the hypothetical evidence as to the eskimoid nature of early Northwest Coast culture, there is an early archeological horizon in the Lower Fraser region which is demonstrably eskimoid in many respects. Whether it can be connected with the predecessors of the modern Coast Salish in the region, or with a Wakashan people, is yet unknown, but the fact that such a culture actually existed near modern Wakashan territory must be considered of outstanding significance.

It is not possible to close this test of our hypothesis with a "quod erat demonstratum"; perhaps future archeological investigations can do that. For the present, however, the hypothesis seems to stand as offering the best available explanation of the distinctive cultural developments on the Northwest Coast and the demonstrated facts of Eskimo-Aleut prehistory.

TABLE I. DISTINCTIVE TRAITS OF NORTHWEST COAST PROVINCES

Northern Province

"Joined" house construction (plates slotted to receive planking)
Rod and slat armor (rod armor also in Northwest California)
Helmets and visors
Puffin beak rattles
Porcupine quill embroidery
"Elbow" adze (some Kwakiutl also)
Heavy splitting adze
One-piece barbed (nontoggling) harpoon points
Hafted stone mauls (also Northern Kwakiutl and Bella Coola)
V-shaped halibut hook
Women's labret (also Northern Kwakiutl)
Men's breechcloth
Occasional use of tailored skin clothing
Leggings (knee-length, ceremonial)
"Northern" canoe type (Kwakiutl also)
Tobacco-chewing with lime
Matrilineal social organization with crests
Displays of clan crests as the principal ceremonial form
Cremation of the dead (rare among Haida; traditionally practiced by Bella Coola)
Highly stylized representative art
Elaborately carved, large, memorial columns ("totem poles")

Wakashan Province

End-thrown sea-hunting harpoons with finger-holes or rests
Curved halibut hook (adjacent Coast Salish also)
"D-shaped" adze (some adjacent Salish also)
Dentalia-fishing (Nootka only)
Sealskin floats for sea mammal hunting
Whaling with lines and floats (Nootka and some adjacent groups)
Ritual use of human corpses and skeletons
Conical olachen net (diffused to northern neighbors)
Harpoon-rest attached to canoe
Lineage-local group organization with no unilateral bias
Dancing societies (subsequently diffused to other groups)
Movable masks, puppets, and similar mechanical devices in ritual
Box burial in caves and trees
Simplified realism in art

Coast Salish-Chinook Province

Mat lodge temporary dwellings
Coiled basketry
Multiple-prong bird dart

Truncated conical basketry cap for women
Duck nets
Dog-wool (and mountain goat wool) checker robes woven on double bar looms
Small steam sweat-lodge
Canoe burial
Loosely defined system of social rank
"Spirit canoe" ceremony
Guardian spirit singing the chief ritual

NORTHWEST CALIFORNIA PROVINCE

Men's house-sweathouse complex with direct fire sweat-bathing
Wooden pillow and stool
Plank dwelling with three-pitch roof
Specialized canoe type
Hemispherical basketry cap for women
Women's chin tattoo
Straight adze
Tobacco smoking (Oregon Coast and Chinook also)
Grinding and leaching of acorns
Featherwork decoration (woodpecker scalps, etc.)
Wealth display ceremonials
"World Renewal" rites
Highly specialized variant of areal shamanistic pattern

TABLE 2.   OVERLAP OF TRAITS BETWEEN PROVINCES TO SHOW INTERPROVINCIAL RELATIONSHIPS

Traits common only to Northern, Wakashan, and Coast Salish-Chinook Provinces
Kerffed and bent wooden boxes
Suspended warp looms ("half-looms") with twined (or twilled twined) woven robes
Basketry hats of conical (or modified conical) shapes
Head-taking in war
Potlatching
Soul-loss an important cause of illness
"Dancing Society" performances (diffused from Wakashan Province)
Grave (and memorial) monuments

Traits common only to Northern, Coast Salish-Chinook, and Northwest California Provinces
Sinew-backed bow (sporadic in Northern Province)
Deerhoof rattles (one of several Northern Province types)

Traits common only to Northern and Wakashan Provinces
Sporadic use of pile dwellings
Nets of minor use in fishing
Urine used as detergent (with ritual connotations) (Gulf of Georgia Salish also)
Rigidity of social ranking (except Bella Coola)
Large-scale warfare, often with economic motivation

Traits common only to Northern and Coast Salish-Chinook Provinces
None

Traits common only to Northern and Northwest California Provinces
    Rod armor
    Tobacco-growing
    Houses with central excavated pit
    Weregild concept stressed

Traits common only to Wakashan, Coast Salish-Chinook, and Northwest California Provinces
    None

Traits common only to Wakashan and Coast Salish-Chinook Provinces
    "Nootkan" type canoe (some Southern Kwakiutl also)
    Detachable plank siding on dwellings (not Chinook and Oregon Coast groups)
    Head deformation (style varied locally)

Traits common only to Wakashan and Northwest California Provinces
    None

Traits common only to Coast Salish-Chinook and Northwest California Provinces
    Large nets important in fishing

NEW ARCHEOLOGICAL INTERPRETATIONS IN NORTHEASTERN SOUTH AMERICA

Clifford Evans

IN RECENT YEARS the accumulation of archeological knowledge about various parts of South America has been tremendous. The majority of this intense work has been devoted to areas where the cultural remains are so lush and spectacular that the archeologist comes away with a wealth of material artifacts. South American areas producing less flashy materials have tended to be ignored. This overabundance of specimens has sometimes caused the archeologist to be so preoccupied with the elaborate descriptions of the artifacts that the real meaning behind them has not always been fully stressed. On the other hand, work in the less rich cultures and in the tropical forest where the climate destroys all the perishable goods, forces the archeologist to squeeze the data for all they are worth and to orient himself immediately toward interpretations of the data in the light of aboriginal cultural development in the whole of South America.

The main function of the archeologist, regardless of his specialized area, is to reconstruct the past cultures—their movements, their development—from the few scraps of data he is able to dig up. In other words, he attempts to derive meaningful interpretations from his data, to reconstruct the past cultures into their positions as living groups at a specific time in history and in certain environmental situations. Recently, in realizing this need of bringing all the anthropological data for the whole of South America and Central America into a meaningful framework, some of our more forward thinking anthropologists have presented various theoretical interpretations on the development of these cultures through time and space. They based their theories upon the best data available at that time.[1] Some of those theories were bound to prove incorrect as field work filled out the tremendous gaps in information that existed in so much of South America; other hypotheses would stand as originally presented and would

---

[1] *The Handbook of South American Indians,* edited by Julian H. Steward went to press beginning in 1944 with Volume 1; the final Volume, 6, was submitted in 1948.

be confirmed by field evidence. The importance of taking the known data and formulating them into interpretations, hypotheses, and theories cannot be overstressed. Instead of merely continuing to collect data from unexplored regions, a series of research problems present themselves as worthy of further investigation. Thus, although some of the theories on the development and movements of aboriginal cultures in South America have recently proved invalid as a result of field work, it must be clearly understood that the original formulation of these theories offered such a challenge for fruitful scientific exploration that they constitute a step forward in anthropological thinking as applied to New World problems. Since the topic of discussion involves some of the newer data that invalidate some of these original formulations, it will be necessary to mention briefly a few of the theories as a background for an understanding of the problems at hand.

While organizing the data for the *Handbook of South American Indians* (Steward, 1946-1950) Julian H. Steward had the difficult problem of finding a system into which the massive amount of ethnological and archeological data could be organized so that it would have meaning. He resolved his problem by arranging the various cultures into culture areas, which he designated as the Marginal Area, the Tropical Forest Area, the Circum-Caribbean Area, and the Andean Area. These categories were the result of grouping together those cultures with similar material traits, social and political structures, religious organizations, patterns of subsistence, etc. Thus, his system formed culture areas which at the same time represented levels of cultural development. Since an understanding of the general characteristics distinguishing the particular stage of cultural development reached in each of these culture areas is essential to the topic of this paper, it will be necessary to define each one briefly.

MARGINAL AREA: Existence depends upon hunting, fishing, and gathering of wild foods with no agriculture. Simple arts and crafts are made by all. There are no specialists and there is a general absence of pottery. The social organization is extremely simple with leaders whose control of the other members of the society is highly limited. Religion is unorganized and on the simple shaman level. The largest socio-political group is the extended family and the pattern of existence is generally nomadic, determined by the food supply.

TROPICAL FOREST AREA: Food gathering is largely supplanted by slash and burn agriculture, although hunting, fishing, and gathering still remain important. This permits larger and more permanent settlements although exhaustion of agricultural lands requires frequent movement of the village. Pottery, loom weaving, and woven basketry are introduced. Social organization remains on the kinship level, with the chief exercising little control. The shaman begins to emerge as a part-time occupational specialist.

CIRCUM-CARIBBEAN AREA: Based upon more productive food resources, this culture is more complex than the Tropical Forest type, particularly in its socio-political and religious aspects. There is a decided divison of labor with a strong development of a priest-temple-idol cult. Strong social, political, and religious leaders arise and social classes make their appearance. Arts and crafts are more highly developed technologically and may be specialized occupations.

ANDEAN AREA: Here, the highest development of cultures in the South American continent was reached. Strong political empires were characterized by a sharp division of labor and a rigid system of social classes. Conquest and expansion were carried out with a well-organized, standing army. Intense agriculture and a wide variety of food plants permitted a high crop yield with the surplus food stored for future use. All arts and crafts reached a high technological development, mass production of textiles, pottery, woodwork, metallurgy, and stone sculpture was typical. Large cities, public works, bridges, roads, and massive irrigation projects developed as a result of planning and an organized system of supervision and work. There was a state religion with a well-organized priesthood.

Although these four types of culture describe areal differences in South America, there is archeological evidence to show that they also correspond to stages of evolution of culture. In Peru, where the outline of development is well known, the sequence begins with hunting, fishing, and gathering cultures living on the coast and in the highlands. After agriculture becomes the main pattern of subsistence and pottery and weaving appear, the culture assumes the general characteristics of the Tropical Forest pattern. With further improvement and expansion of agricultural facilities, towns grew larger, social organization became more formalized, arts and crafts became the work of specialists, and religion was served by priests, all of which is comparable to the level of development achieved in the Circum-Caribbean Area. The climax in Peru was higher, however, and this is the aspect of Andean culture emphasized in the description of the Andean Culture Area. In other words, the culture area division provided by Steward also holds the connotation of levels or stages of cultural development, leading from simplicity to complexity.

One other point is worthy of clarification before launching into the theme of the paper. The environmental limitation on culture is a factor that will be demonstrated to be of essential importance when examining the particular level to which a culture has developed or declined. For example, it is not accidental that the Andean Area with its fertile coastal desert lands and rich intermontane valleys was the part of South America where culture reached its highest development. Such development could not have occurred in the Amazon drainage because of the impossibility of achieving the prerequisite, which is intensive agriculture. It will be demonstrated that environment has had an important effect in limiting the development of culture in northeastern South America and that in the light of archeo-logical evidence, the role of environment becomes an integral part of the whole picture and not just the setting (cf. Meggers, 1954).

With this brief summary of the levels of cultural development in South America, we can now indicate a few of the theories that were arrived at largely on the basis of ethnographical distribution and historical evidence, with little or no information available from archeological sources. The more important of these theories are:

1. The Amazon was settled by a Circum-Caribbean type of culture which moved eastward along the northern coast of South America and then southward to the mouth of the Amazon where it spread up the river and into its tributaries and in the process deteriorated into the Tropical Forest or the Marginal level of development (Steward, 1948, p. 885; 1949a, p. 762).

2. Marajó Island in the mouth of the Amazon River was the place of origin of the elaborate Marajoara culture, which had a highly developed pottery art utilizing excision (called by some "champlevé") and elaborate painting, urn burial, and artificial mounds. After development here, the Marajoara influences are supposed to have moved south along the coast of Brazil and then inland to the Paraná drainage; upriver, spreading into the lowlands of Bolivia and the eastern Montaña; and northward, along the coast of the mainland into the Guianas and into the Lesser Antilles (Steward, 1948, p. 885 and Willey, 1949, Map 3 and p. 196).

3. "Because the Guianas have the greatest number of traits regarded as characteristic of the Tropical Forests, they may be postulated as a center of dispersal . . ." of Tropical Forest Culture (Steward, 1948, p. 886).

4. Although not in the same category as the above scientific theories, we might mention the famous theory dating back to Sir Walter Raleigh's and Spanish times of the 16th century when such vivid

stories were circulated about the lost civilization of "El Dorado" in the interior of what is today known as British Guiana. Although these "El Dorado" myths and their many variations had been debunked many times, there are a few diehards who cling hopefully to the thought that some day the archeologists will uncover those hidden riches said to equal the civilizations of ancient Mexico and Peru.

With this background, let us now review briefly the results of arche-ological fieldwork in the Territory of Amapá (Brazilian Guiana), on the Islands of Mexiana, Caviana, and Marajó (Evans and Meggers, 1950; Meggers and Evans, ms) and in British Guiana (Evans and Meggers, n.d.), supplemented by information derived from collections of archeological speci-mens from the Amazon and Orinoco drainages. It is not within the scope of this discussion to describe in detail the various potsherds, the complexes of pottery, the design styles and elements, and the specific traits of each area, but the reader is assured that the statements made can be fully sub-stantiated by the details which normally accompany any archeological report. The interested student can look up these reports, seek the final monographs when they appear, and juggle the data to suit himself; however, it is absolutely guaranteed that generalizations or interpretative statements are not made here without supporting evidence based upon extensive strati-graphic excavations, seriational studies, and comparative analyses.

Let us summarize the results of these studies and see how they affect the various theories set forth in the first part of this paper. Stratigraphic excavations on the Islands of Marajó, Mexiana, and Caviana have revealed that instead of the elaborate pottery, urn burial, and mound complex of the Marajoara[2] being the result of gradual local development out of simpler groups, it was preceded and followed by simpler cultures which were totally unrelated to it. In other words, there is not a single bit of evidence to indicate that this complex culture, with its specialized division of labor, social stratification, and a highly developed pottery art, originated on the Islands in the mouth of the Amazon. Quite contrary to both Steward's and Willey's reconstruction, instead of Marajó Island being the point of origin and a center of dispersal for this elaborate culture, the Marajoara is a late culture already highly developed when it arrived.

Let us pursue further the point that the Islands in the mouth of the Amazon may have served as the place of origin of any particular aboriginal group. The archeological sequence presents a series of three cultures which precede the Marajoara, none of which grows directly out of the previous

---

[2] This name has been selected to label the mound-building culture on Marajó Island and to distinguish it from the other archeological cultures.

ones. Instead, each archeological horizon appears to be the result of a group of people with a distinct set of traits arriving in the area and either amalga-mating with those groups already here, settling in an unoccupied part of the Islands, conquering, or pushing out the existing inhabitants. Each of these three distinct groups is quite typical and representative of the Tropical Forest level of culture. Their existence on Marajó, Mexiana, and Caviana or any of the nearby regions would not be out of place. In fact, it is exactly what one would expect of the archeological situation from the ethnological evidence of living Indian tribes in the Amazon drainage—small villages, simple cultures, no strong political or social organization, no social classes, simple pottery, arts and crafts made by all and not by a group of specialists.

In the light of comparative ethnological and archeological evidence for the Tropical Forest Area, we can demonstrate that the Marajoara Culture is something completely out of line with the level of cultural development of the archeological horizons which precede and follow it on the Islands. It had no counterpart in any living tribes in this area when the Europeans first contacted the region in 1500 A.D. What makes this Marajoara Culture appear so peculiar in this Tropical Forest context? Why do we say so posi-tively that it did not grow out of the simpler cultures of the Tropical Forest level of development which preceded it? The reasons are several:

1. The pottery reveals a development in technique, design, and form far superior to that found in the Tropical Forest cultures and must be compared to the Circum-Caribbean or Sub-Andean stage of cultural development.

2. The construction of artificial mounds, both burial and habitation, is the result of organized manpower and not merely the haphazard accumulation of dirt according to the individual whim of separate families. These structures had to be built by laborers, supervised and managed, whose full time could be spent in this type of construction work, while others raised food to support these workers, their super-visors, the ruler, etc. In other words, a stratified society is indicated, and this conclusion is substantiated by the presence of differential treatment of the dead.

3. The distinctive Marajoara culture traits do not occur in any of the earlier archeological horizons in the Lower Amazon area.

4. Within the Marajoara Culture itself, there is evidence that the culture arrived full blown and at the peak of its achievement and that it thereafter began slowly to decline to the Tropical Forest level.

In other words, our archeological data show that the one example of the Circum-Caribbean or Sub-Andean level of culture in the Lower Amazon

is not an indigenous development, and further that it was unable to maintain this higher culture after its resettlement in the new environment.

This evidence supports Steward's (1949a, pp. 760-3) conclusion that
a culture of the Circum-Caribbean level of development will decline when
transplanted into the tropical forest environment, and clearly reveals the
limitations of that type of environment for cultural development. A culture
with an advanced socio-political system including social stratification and
occupational division of labor can exist only when population is concentrated. A prerequisite to population concentration is a permanent and productive food supply. This is not available in the tropical forest environment,
where the relatively small area of cultivatable land and the natural poverty
of the soil require the constant clearing of new fields and the abandonment
of those of the year before.[3] Fields are scattered and constantly must be
moved and the villages have the same characteristics. The effect of this
type of subsistence pattern on a culture with higher requirements is well
illustrated in the fate of the Marajoara Culture on Marajó Island. When
the constant and abundant food supply to which it was adjusted in its
original habitat was removed, the prop was knocked away and the whole
culture fell apart. As the labor required to secure an adequate food supply
increased, specialized craftsmen had to leave their work to join the hunt.
With the downfall of occupational specialization came a breakdown in the
basis for social stratification and apparently a decline in the necessity for
strong leadership. By the time the next group arrived on Marajó Island,
the once elaborate culture had been reduced to the Tropical Forest level
of development, which is adjusted to the subsistence limitations set by the
local environment.

If neither the Marajoara Culture nor any of the four Tropical Forest
cultural horizons developed on Marajó, Mexiana, and Caviana, but instead
came into the Islands from some other place, the next question is: "From
where did they come?" If South American archeology today were as well
known as some other parts of the New World, perhaps the answer would
be an easy one. Instead, only suggestions exist for there are still great areas
of South America that are totally unexplored from an archeological standpoint. However, negative evidence helps eliminate certain directions of
movement or sources. Since the four earliest archeological horizons on the
Islands have no affiliations in the Territory of Amapá, in the Guianas, in
the Lesser and Greater Antilles, or in the Lower Orinoco, their source does
not appear to be in this direction. If the settlement of the Amazon was by

---

[3] For an excellent discussion of the problems of slash and burn agriculture,
the decreasing productivity of the field with each year's planting, and the size of fields
necessary to produce certain amounts of manioc, see Wagley, 1953, pp. 67-71.

a movement around the north coast and down the east coast of South America and then up the Amazon River, surely there would be some evidence of these various cultures between the Amazon and Central America or the Antilles. There is not one bit of related material. Our excavations in the Territory of Amapá and in British Guiana, Rouse's and Cruxent's in the Lower Orinoco and Trinidad (Personal Communication), as well as Goethal's in Dutch Guiana (ms), and the reported aboriginal pottery from French Guiana have revealed cultural materials that do not correlate with any of the aforementioned cultural horizons on any of the Islands in the mouth of the Amazon. If they did move from the north around the coast and down to the mouth of the Amazon, these aboriginal peoples were in a nonstop dugout trip that would rival the best nonstop jet plane or steamship schedule today. The small amount of evidence which can be gleaned from the extremely sparse ethnological and archeological data suggests that the major direction of movement of these cultures is downriver from the headwaters of the Amazon and its numerous tributaries. This suggests the origin point as somewhere in the eastern parts of Ecuador, Colombia, and Peru.

There is evidence, however, that the coastal route from the north around the mainland was used once. This was by the Aruã, the last group to settle at the mouth of the Amazon and the one occupying the Islands at the time of the European discovery in 1500 A.D. Our archeological sequences in the Territory of Amapá and on Caviana, Mexiana, and Marajó as well as comparative data from the Antillean regions indicate that the Aruã moved from the north, probably out of the Lesser Antilles, into the Territory of Amapá where they stopped only briefly before going over into the Islands of Caviana and Mexiana and the north coast of Marajó. In other words, the only evidence of a cultural movement along the mainland and around the northeastern coast of South America is a late one, occurring about 1300-1400 A.D. Such evidence is not sufficient to postulate this route as the main direction of cultural movement into and up the Amazon.

Thus, several complete changes have been made in the postulated origins and directions of cultural movements into the Tropical Forest areas:

1. The Island of Marajó is not the place of origin or development of any of the archeological cultures that have been discovered there.

2. Neither did this Island act as a center of dispersal from which cultures or culture traits diffused either to the mainland or up river.

3. The elaborate Marajoara culture of Marajó Island is not indigenous and it represents a higher level of development than the Tropical Forest Cultures, apparently achieved somewhere in eastern Ecuador and Colombia (Meggers and Evans, ms).

89

4. The Marajoara Culture arrived on the Island at the peak of its development and then began a decline to the simpler Tropical Forest level.

5. The explanation for this decline can be found in the limitations of the tropical forest environment, which does not permit the intensive agricultural production resulting in high yield per man-hour of output that is essential for the continuing support of an advanced level of cultural development.

6. Only the latest culture, which reached the mouth of the Amazon about 1300-1400 A.D., shows evidence of having come down the coast from the north.

7. All of the other cultures that can be traced appear to have moved down the Amazon and its tributaries, suggesting that the main movement of migration and diffusion took this route from west to east.

In order to test the thesis proposed by Steward (1948, p. 886) that the Tropical Forest Pattern of culture developed in the Guianas and diffused from there to other parts of lowland South America, we carried the search for evidence into the Guianas. If this interpretation, which was based upon the great diversity of traits found ethnographically in the area, is correct, then the archeological record should show a long history of occupation by cultures of this type, or at least a longer one than can be detected at the mouth of the Amazon. A greater antiqutiy in the place of origin is necessary to allow for the time lapse involved in diffusion from this center. However, our survey and excavation of 95 sites distributed over British Guiana failed to produce any evidence that Tropical Forest culture originated in this part of South America. Almost without exception, the pottery-producing archeological horizons of British Guiana, whether on the coast or in the interior, are relatively late, that is, at most just a few hundred years before 1500 A.D. In fact, the sites of the Rupununi District in the far interior are so late that they are probably all post 1500 A.D.

Not only did these sites in the interior of British Guiana prove to be late in the time sequence for South America as a whole, but there was no evidence of any sort to suggest that high civilizations with elaborate arts and crafts, especially metal work, reminiscent of the vivid imaginary description of El Dorado ever existed in the interior of British Guiana. In fact, we explored the borders of several lakes in the interior of British Guiana that are supposed to be the sites of El Dorado and the best that could be found was one or two plain, insignificant and uninspiring potsherds of the same late horizons as were typical of the whole area. What is known of

Dutch and French Guiana, as well as Brazilian Guiana, supports these same conclusions.

In a summary of the work in British Guiana, as well as comparative information from the other Guianas, several basic points can be made:

1. In the absence of any time depth to the archeological horizons in the Guianas, this area cannot be considered the place of develop-ment of the Tropical Forest cultures.

2. With the exception of a few preceramic shell mounds, all the archeological evidence in British Guiana indicates that the region was settled by semisedentary agriculturists of the Tropical Forest level of culture only a short time before European contact in 1500 A.D., with the majority of the aboriginal groups moving into the area after this date.

3. There is no archeological evidence to support the mythological stories of high aboriginal cultures in the Guianas, identified by the early writers as El Dorado.

Since this appears to be the situation, how can it be explained? Why does this part of the Guianas show even less depth of aboriginal occupation than do the Islands at the mouth of the Amazon? What caused the great variety of cultural traits to be found on the ethnographic horizon? Since the area is not a point of origin but instead appears to be a place of refuge, does the archeological evidence suggest the place or places from which these cultures might have come?

Although the archeological evidence of the Guianas does not indicate a long period of habitation by cultures of the Tropical Forest type, we cannot assume that this means the area was totally uninhabited prior to this time. Just enough scattered finds of preceramic, hunting and gathering peoples do occur to suggest that the area was sporadically populated with Indians of the Marginal level of culture who lived by fishing and gathering and who constantly moved around following the food supplies, never set-tling in large villages or in any one place for any great length of time. Compared with other regions of South America, the environmental oppor-tunities in the Guianas for a Marginal type of culture to subsist on hunting wild game, gathering wild foods, fishing, and collecting shell fish are not particularly good nor bad. However, when you consider the next step upwards in the stage of cultural development in South America, that is, the Tropical Forest cultures, the situation in the Guianas becomes gen-erally unfavorable.

From superficial examination of a map showing the geographical fea-tures of the Guianas, one would conclude that the area is just as good as many other parts of the tropical forest for an aboriginal group practicing slash and burn agriculture. Actually, this is not true, but the realization comes only after intimate contact with the land. The coastal area is swampy and other areas are subject to flooding in the rainy season. The savanna of the interior of British Guiana and adjacent Brazil is useful only to a modern cattle economy and then questionably so compared to other grazing lands in the world; it cannot be used successfully for agriculture. Suitable agricultural land adjoining rivers is not abundant because of the unevenness of the terrain, alternating small hills with low lands that completely flood during the height of the rainy season, leaving a very small percentage of land available for slash and burn agriculture. Since slash and burn agriculture in a tropical rain forest requires the moving of the field every 2 to 5 years and the land does not renew its vitality for numerous decades, the arable land can actually be exhausted in a relatively short period. From a careful ground study of the Upper Essequibo region of British Guiana, we calculated that only 10 percent of the area is actually potentially usable for slash and burn agriculture, thus limiting the number of people and the length of time they can stay in this area. If an abundance of Pre-Cambrian granite and tons of fluvial white sand would make an area potentially habitable, British Guiana would have been the garden spot of aboriginal South America for it has an overabundance of these two features. But when considered as a whole, this was as poor an area for permanent habitation by aboriginal man as it is today, where even 20th century techniques have increased the usable agricultural land only in coastal areas that have been reclaimed from the sea by a large-scale system of dikes, economically feasible only because they were built originally in the days of slave labor.

Although these comments are based upon intimate familiarity with the ground conditions of British Guiana and Brazilian Guiana (Territory of Amapá), a check with other scientists and an examination of the literature indicates that the descriptions also fit the conditions of French Guiana, Dutch Guiana, the southeastern extremes of Venezuela, and the portions of the interior of Brazil which border this whole region. In other words, from a geographical standpoint the area known as the Guianas is a broader concept than the modern political divisions. Without laboring the point any further, there appears to be no doubt that this region was less conducive to permanent settlement by the Indians than were many other parts of South America. Interestingly, the geographical features also affected the easy acceptance of the area by Europeans who at first settled more intensely along the Orinoco and Amazon Rivers. Even today the swampy coastland, the heavy jungle, the rivers and streams with rapids every few miles, the steep and rugged forested mountains, and extremely infertile soil have attracted few European settlers. For example, the interior of British Guiana was not settled by Europeans until as late as 1850, parts of the interior of Dutch Guiana served as a refuge for escaping African slaves throughout the 19th century, some of the major streams in the Guianas today have no one living on them except in the mouths, and such areas as the headwaters of the Essequibo, Mapuera, New, Courantyne, and Alto Trombetas Rivers are inhabited only by a few unacculturated Indian groups with only an occasional missionary settlement.

Actually, the Guianas not only served as a refuge into which the Indians could pour and escape the whites at the time of first European contact in South America in 1500 A.D., but this area is still serving as one of the last regions undisturbed by white man where aboriginal groups can live relatively uncontaminated by modern westernized cultures. Historically, we can trace these movements from the present day backward in time with various sorts of evidence—archive documents, linguistics, and archeology. The archeological data are not as complete as is desirable for two reasons: (1) Much of northern South America is still not thoroughly explored from an archeological standpoint; and (2) as these various groups were disrupted from their original settlements and their culture began to suffer the shock of culture contact with the Europeans, there was often such a breakdown in the arts and crafts, especially the pottery technology, that it is extremely difficult to relate the archeological evidence with the ethnographic data from tribes living in this region or in nearby areas.

The archeology of the Rupununi District of the interior of British Guiana and the adjoining Territory of Rio Branco in Brazil indicates that these areas were settled very recently (within the last few hundred years) by the same group of Indians. In fact, even today there is free movement back and forth by the Indians, who are now completely acculturated. The habitation sites in the headwaters of the Essequibo River and some of the upper reaches of the Orinoco River are all of relatively recent deposition, and suggest groups pushing back into areas to get away from regions of more intense European occupation. In fact, even today the Indians along the tributaries of the north side of the Amazon River are pushing farther and farther up the streams and in one case, in the extreme southern part of British Guiana, a tribe has moved from Brazil into the headwaters of the Essequibo River only within the last 20 to 25 years. Historical evidence clearly demonstrates the shifts and movements of various tribes of Indians from along the main water routes, such as the Amazon, the Orinoco, and the coast, to the more remote parts of the Amazon and Orinoco drainages. The Aruã moved out of the Islands at the mouth of the Amazon to the mainland, especially into French Guiana. In fact, the linguistic distribution

93

in the interior of British Guiana today is concrete evidence of the recent influx of different tribes, producing a very peculiar and spotty distribution of Arawak and Carib speaking tribes.

Thus, the Guianas, instead of being a point of origin for the Tropical Forest Cultures, turn out to be a refuge into which the nearby tribes retreated to get away from the Europeans. Steward's postulation that the Guianas were a center of dispersal because this area "had the greatest number of traits regarded as characteristic of the Tropical Forests" (Steward, 1948, p. 886) actually can be turned around to mean something else on the basis of archeological, ethnological, and linguistic data. His observation that the area had the greatest number of typical Tropical Forest culture traits is a sound one and this diversity becomes even more understandable when it is seen as the result of events that brought into the area tribes from all parts of the Amazon and Orinoco where different varieties of the general cultural pattern had developed.

The conclusions of our research, presented here briefly and without the detailed factual support, completely contradict several previously proposed interpretations of the origin and dispersal of culture in northeastern South America. Since the evidence is basically derived from archeological excavations and from comparative studies of archeological traits in other areas, the vitality of the conclusions can be tested by the manner in which they fit the total environmental and cultural picture in South America. It has been pointed out that the tropical forest environment seems to set a limitation on the level to which a culture exploiting it can develop. The conclusion that the elaborate Marajoara Culture is not indigenous to the mouth of the Amazon is in accord with this environmental evidence, and could have been predicted on the basis of it. The long-held theorem of diffusion—that dispersion tends to be outward in all directions from the center of development—is better reflected in the reconstruction of the major movements as coming eastward down the rivers and ultimately working their way to the Atlantic coast than if we try to visualize a route eastward through Venezuela, south of the mouth of the Amazon, and then westward again to the foot of the Andes. Finally, the conclusion that the Guianas constituted a refuge rather than a place where the Tropical Forest type of culture first developed is supported by archive records since prehistory gave way to history in northeastern South America.

THE NEW ORIENTATION TOWARD PROBLEMS OF ASIATIC-AMERICAN RELATIONSHIPS

Gordon F. Ekholm

THE NEW ORIENTATION referred to in the title of this paper is not meant to be a promise of some entirely fresh light on the problems mentioned. It refers rather to what I detect in the writings of many Americanists during the last few years of an awakening of interest in the possibility that the native American cultures may have been influenced by those of the Old World to a somewhat greater extent than has been believed in the recent past. My intent is to comment variously on this trend and its future significance to American anthropology and in so doing to make as explicit as possible my own views on this particular aspect of our inquiries into the origin and development of the American Indian cultures.

Speaking of a new orientation presupposes an old one, but it is hardly necessary to explain or define this at any length. We all know that for many years it has been tacitly accepted as one of the basic tenets of Americanist studies that everything above the level of the simpler cultures such as could have existed at an early time in the subarctic regions of Siberia and Alaska was independently invented or developed in the New World. We have proceeded to study American Indian history with this as a basic assumption and have trained our students to look no further. It is a position that has been taken for granted in most archeological reports, but is discussed or stated in many others—not as a problem but as an attempt to enhance the rationale of the work. Thus we often read that archeological researches in the Americas have an especial value because they deal with an example of culture history isolated from the main stream of culture history in the Old World.

What questioning there has been of this overriding belief in American isolationism has come mainly from amateur anthropologists or those not trained in American schools. Many of these questionings have been attacked very severely and at best have been labeled as of the "romantic school." We have had the so-called diffusion controversy and more by weight of numbers on the "independent-inventionist" side, it seems to me, we have overly discredited the "diffusionists." There is nothing worse than to be

95

labeled an extreme diffusionist, while most of us, I firmly believe, have become something on the order of extreme independent-inventionists. I think I see a strong bias in this direction in the writings of most American archeologists. It has been apparent not only in our attitude toward the question of extra-American contacts, but in the way we think about things in our own area as well. The burden of proof appears to rest with unfair weight upon the person who would postulate the diffusion of traits from one subarea to another. Most of us have specialized in particular subareas, like Mexico or the Southeast, and few have ventured to develop the subject of the diffusional processes involved in the obvious historical connections of these or other areas. The very important problems of Andean-Mesoamerican relationships are just being outlined, and there have been few speculative schemes for American culture growth as a whole. Personally I feel that we have not maintained a proper balance between these alternative poles of interpretation which are inherent in any attempt at archeological culture-historical reconstruction.

Within the last few years, however, American archeologists, like those in many other fields of science, have felt the need to examine critically the theoretical bases of their work and at the same time to synthesize the knowledge they have accumulated and to make it meaningful in larger contexts. As a result of this there seems to be, as I stated at the beginning, an increasing number of us who would see definite problems in the field of Asiatic-American culture relationships or at least are in a frame of mind to consider the existence of such problems. I find this in conversation with my colleagues and in reviews and articles and even in my being asked to address a meeting of the Anthropological Society of Washington on the subject, something which could not or would not have happened ten years ago. In fact, I am rather amazed at the reaction there has been to the several occasions when I have extended my neck rather invitingly both in an exhibit[1] and in print. I may realize better than anyone else, perhaps, how vulnerable my head is on a number of counts but, nevertheless, no one has seriously swung an axe and I have not been publicly snubbed to any extent. Actually, I think there are many who would like to chop but who hesitate because of an insidious suspicion that *he could be right*.

There are a great many aspects to a consideration of the problems of Asiatic-American relationships and the total subject can be little more than touched upon here. After several more general statements regarding my personal attitude toward the subject, I shall try to organize my comments

---

[1] "Across the Pacific," an exhibit in the American Museum of Natural History prepared by Robert Heine-Geldern, Junius Bird, the writer, and others for the 29th International Congress of Americanists in 1949. For a paper resulting from the preparation of this exhibit see Heine-Geldern and Ekholm, 1951.

by first indicating why I think there are problems and then attempt some suggestions on how these problems can be attacked and understood.

In speaking of Asiatic-American relationships I do not mean only relationships resulting from trans-Pacific or overseas contacts. I include also influences that might have passed through the Bering Straits region, either overland or coastwise, and, of course, those beyond what we have been accustomed to think of as having come across with the earliest migrants or as having come through the known cultures of that region.

Other than a somewhat greater respect than is current for primitive and early civilized men's abilities as travelers, and for the process of diffusion, I have no overall scheme or controlling theory concerning the route or means of Asiatic-American contacts. I am interested in culture-historical problems and in investigating the question of to *what extent* the American cultures were dependent upon those of the Old World. I definitely do not envisage all and every important element of American Indian culture as having been derived from outside sources. Continual change is characteristic of all cultures or civilizations and, although the rate of change varies from group to group, cultures anywhere, where conditions are right, might evolve into more complex forms. Isolated cultural entities must certainly on occasion develop similar patterns of life or even very specifically similar elements, so it is very possible that the American civilizations are to a large extent a product of their own making. On the other hand, however, the processes of one culture stimulating changes in another, of imitation, or diffusion are also always in operation both in simple and in very complex and subtle ways. An entire civilization, for instance, may appear to have developed all by itself, yet might have been dependent for its existence on basic ideas derived from other centers of civilization.

The first and perhaps the outstanding reason why the problems of Asiatic-American relationships are important is one we can all agree on. The several civilizations of Eurasia undoubtedly developed interrelatedly and the only possibility of an entirely separate and independent development of the same kind is in the civilizations of America. So, from the points of view of the philosophy of history, of culture theory, or of many aspects of the science of man and culture, it is important that we investigate the question of whether or not these were independent developments. If we are interested in the history of culture generally, the problems of Asiatic-American relationships are among the most significant ones with which American archeologists have to deal.

A more direct reason why I question the standard isolationist line is that the first of the higher cultures in the Americas appeared at approximately the right time to be explained as a result of diffusion. This is most

MESOPOTAMIA	INDIA	CHINA	AMERICAS
			1500 B.C.
		3000 B.C.	
	4000 B.C.		
5000 B.C.			

FIG. 5. APPROXIMATE DATES OF THE APPEARANCE OF
AGRICULTURE AND POTTERY MAKING.

easily seen in the chart in Figure 5. The outstandingly important complex
of agriculture, pottery making, and the sedentary life would seem to have
begun in the Near East and to have spread outward from there, arriving
in India and China several thousand years later. In the New World, we
place the origin of this stage at about 2000 or 1500 B.C., and this seems
to have come at just about the right time in relation to the others to be
explained on a diffusional basis. If purely independent invention and development is involved, and we don't rely on some physical evolutionary process
as being a contributing cause of such developments, we might wonder at the
timing. Why, we might ask, did the beginning of this agricultural stage not
come at 5000 B.C., at 1000 A.D., or not at all in the New World?

Now, certainly, I do not hold that this is proof of the diffusion of
this pattern of life, but I do think it is one of the contributing reasons why
we should be very much interested in the problems we are considering.

A more disturbing factor to most Americanists has been the apparent
lack of real developmental stages leading from the primitive to the early
civilizational level in the New World sequences. With the excavation of
Huaca Prieta in Peru (Fig. 1) this argument has lost some of its clarity,
but at least in Mesoamerica the earliest documented archeological horizons,
outside of the scattered finds of primitive early man, show the presence
of agriculture, a sedentary village life, and well-developed pottery making

98

traditions obviously some distance from the stage of a first experimentation with the firing of clay.

One cannot be certain, of course, that the apparent lack of adequate developmental stages is not just a function of incomplete archeological testing. Those who feel convinced of the independent origin of the American civilizations point out a number of areas that have not been properly surveyed and insist that the remains of the developmental stages will yet be found. This we must admit is true and possible, but we must be careful, too, that if and when we find what seem to be developmental stages they are not just the beginning stages of the adoption of ideas from other sources. Pottery making, for instance, cannot be adopted outright and immediately by a non-pottery making group. There will be a period of experimentation with the idea which, if we do not have an unusually complete archeological record, will have the appearance of a primary development. A good example of this is the very crude unfired pottery described by Morris for a late Basket Maker horizon and suggested as a possible claim for the invention of pottery making in the southwestern United States. It is now fairly certain that good pottery was being made in neighboring areas and that this must have been an attempt at its imitation (Morris, 1927).

We do not have the space here to discuss this particular point at greater length. Speaking very generally, I can only say that our not having found developmental stages in the New World is far from being direct proof that Asiatic influences are involved—but it is a contributing factor suggesting the need for an open mind toward the possibility of extra-American origins.

In the past, the supposed strict dichotomy of the cultivated plants of the Old and New Worlds has been thought to be sufficient indication that the culture histories of the two areas were quite separate from each other. Now, however, we find this conclusion questioned on several counts, and it is very possible that the study of cultivated plants will be the most important factor in proving the reality of Asiatic-American cultural relationships. Plant species are not something that can be invented by man, so the occurrence of particular species as domesticates in two portions of the world is more definite indication of historical contacts than are purely cultural items. In looking into this matter we are largely, of course, in the hands of the specialists—the botanists—and we are fortunate in having a number of these who are very much interested in the problems of American plant origins.

The botanists seem to have taken sides on the matter of trans-Pacific contacts, but those who are opposed have apparently not been able to explain away successfully the genetic evidence that the New World cottons are a cross between an Asiatic cultivated variety and a wild American form and that the transfer of the first was most likely accomplished through man's agency (Hutchinson, Silow, and Stephens, 1947; Silow, 1953). It is necessary to affirm, however, that in considering this evidence we must proceed with caution, for even for the most diffusionist-minded of us it is somewhat difficult to conceive of trans-Pacific crossings as early as 2000 B.C. But Oceanic and American distributions have been claimed for other plants (Carter, 1950), and there is the old reliable sweet potato which everyone seems to agree was transported from America to Polynesia in pre-European times.

The study of cultivated plants is a complex one and requires much more research, but I think we can fairly say that current knowledge of the subject calls again for an open mind in the matter of Asiatic-American relationships. We must continue to gather the evidence there is on the history of plant cultivation and by cooperating with and posing problems for the botanists goad them on to further research.

The final category of things which are indicative of problems in the field of Asiatic-American relationships includes the many parallels in customs, beliefs, technical processes, styles, and motifs occurring on the two sides of the Pacific, which have often been considered singly or together as proof of historical contacts. I cannot list and discuss these in any systematic way and, while mentioning only some of them, shall concern myself primarily with the principles involved in judging their significance to the subject we are considering.

As we all know, we find strong differences of opinion as to the meaning of these cultural parallels, there being those who emphasize the importance of diffusion and those who emphasize the inventiveness of man and the probability that the same things will be developed independently again and again given the proper environmental and social conditions. The whole problem has not been considered very seriously, and much of the discussion pro and con has had the flavor of legalistic argument with those on each side trying to prove their already established convictions. Some of the objections to the thesis that contacts did occur are basically sound and give us important leads as to how the matter should be investigated, but we should note that others have no real validity.

Some examples of these questionable arguments might be mentioned. Mainly, they concern the absences of certain traits in the New World cultures with the assumption that if significant contacts had occurred they would have been present. The lack of the use of the wheel is often cited but this to me is far from being proof that contacts did not occur. The wheel was not used very extensively in most portions of eastern Asia, and it is, furthermore, unlikely that the idea of the use of the wheel would have certainly resulted in its adoption by peoples, like the Mexicans, who had already established very successful ways of getting along without it. They had no domesticated animals readily adaptable to draft purposes and the adoption would have required the establishment of special forms of carpentry and the building of roads. Even with the Spanish Conquest, when Mexico was completely dominated by a wheel-using culture, the use of the wheel took over very slowly. One still sees the Indians back-packing heavy loads for great distances along modern paved highways. It has often been said that the pyramids of Middle America could not be related to those of the Old World because they are built as bases for temples and not in the manner of the Egyptian pyramids as burial monuments. The answer is, of course, that the pyramids of Egypt are a specialized development and that pyramidal structures supporting shrines and temples are common in Mesopotamia and in greater India. The same applies to supposed major differences in agricultural techniques—the broadcast sowing of grain in the Old World and the use of horticultural techniques in the New. The latter are also dominant in eastern Asia.

Among the more serious objections to considering the various cultural parallels as being evidence of diffusion from Asia to America are those based upon chronology. Many who have claimed diffusion as being responsible for certain parallels have not always paid sufficient regard to this obvious necessity. We cannot even discuss this in general terms here except to insist that each particular item must be considered in the light of what we know of the time of its origin in both of the areas and to note that for the most part there seems to be no basic difficulty .The sequence of developmental stages seems to have followed its course somewhat later in America than in Asia as a whole and, in the main, things in America seem to be rather later than too early. This is dependent also upon the accuracy of the chronological schemes for our two areas which, it must always be remembered, are subject to adjustment.

Another objection to seeing Asiatic influence in America is the sup-posed lack of any logical order or patterning of those elements which might have been imported, that they are found to be scattered among the New World cultures, appearing at differing times and in cultures of varying degrees of development and not presenting a pattern which could have resulted from specific kinds of contacts at specific times. And, looking at the evidence in a casual way, as we have tended to do, these objections have seemed to be valid ones.

But I am inclined to think that this seeming confusion may be more apparent than real and that when we seriously look for some patterning in the various elements of possible Asiatic origin we will find it to exist. In complex phenomena of this kind, a meaningful order or arrangement of the component parts will not appear by itself; it has to be dug out and seen in accordance with some theoretical construct or belief that it might exist. In other words, we must give the idea a chance and not begin with the assumption that it is an impossibility. Obviously, this will become more and more possible with every advance in our knowledge of American and Asiatic culture history.

Recently, I attempted to make a start toward bringing this kind of order into some of the many motifs and elements of style in Mayan and Mexican ceremonial art which are reminiscent of things in India and southeast Asia (Ekholm, 1953). I postulated what I called Complex A, consisting of a number of traits which seem to appear in Mesoamerica toward the end of the Classic Period at about 700 A.D., or shortly thereafter, many of which continued in use until the time of the Spanish Conquest. These traits having Asiatic counterparts are found to exist in the unusual sculptural style of Palenque, at late Classic sites in northern Yucatan, and in Mexican Period Chichen Itzá. Some of them also occur in the Mixteca-Puebla area and into the Toltec and Axtec cultures of central Mexico, all of the cultures in which they are represented being obviously related in a number of ways. Perhaps the most striking Asiatic-American parallels in this series are the lotus panels of Palenque and Chichen Itzá and those of Amarāvati and other sites in India, the use of the serpent balustrade and serpent column in Chichen Itzá and in Java, and the unique "Asiatic" manner in which the relief sculptures of Palenque are drawn. This was a trial balloon, and traits have probably been included which are not convincingly enough like their counterparts in Asia, but I feel certain that the postulation contains some modicum of reality and can be elaborated upon and perfected.

This kind of study was difficult for me, as it would be to most ordinary American archeologists, for it requires making oneself acquainted to some extent with the entirely new and extremely complex field of Asiatic art and archeology. The materials dealt with are also of the kind which belong more properly in the history of art field than in anthropology. The subject needs students trained along both of these lines as well as in the art and architecture of Middle America before it can be thoroughly developed. This would be valuable not only for the light it might throw on Asiatic-American relationships; comparative studies of the higher cultures of America and the early civilizations of the Old World would be of the greatest importance in other ways, I believe, to Americanist studies.

I suspect that it will eventually be possible to visualize other complexes of things suggestive of Asiatic origins in the cultures of the earlier periods of the Mesoamerican sequence, but as yet I am not ready to do so. The principal difficulty lies in the relatively meager knowledge we have of the content of these earlier cultures and the confusing problems of their relative dating in the several subareas. Some things appearing in the latter part of the pre-Classic Period or the beginning of the Classic, in the era between 500 B.C. and the time of Christ, are the temple pyramid complex and various associated elements of building techniques and plans which find their counterparts in the Near East and distributed on into India. The early pyramid tombs of the Miraflores period in Highland Guatemala have an unusual resemblance to the Shang tombs of China. There are some portions of the Maya calendrical and writing systems, as well as certain religious and cosmological concepts, whose independent origin one might question. Dating to this general period also is the beginning of the Tajín style of decoration which, on a number of counts, is remarkably like the designs on Late Chou objects of China. I make absolutely no claims for these things at the present time, and mention them only to give an idea of the kinds of things that might be included in the formulation of an earlier complex.

Another curious combination of items of a still earlier period interests me greatly, but for these too I will make no claims. At Tlatilco in Central Mexico, a site of the pre-Classic Period, we find along with well-developed pottery an abundance of clay figurines and clay stamps or seals, both roller stamps and flat ones. Clay figurines of a "mother goddess," or fertility-cult type can be understood as a functionally derived independent development, but I find it hard to believe that stamps or seals could be expected in a like manner. Clay figurines and seals are, of course, common to the early cultures of both the Near East and of the Indus Valley areas. Could this be part of a still earlier complex in which the ideas of agriculture and pottery making were introduced into the New World?

Another group of interesting parallels suggesting Asiatic-American relationships are certain traits which are known archeologically but have the added advantage for the purposes of our study in having persisted into modern times and are known historically and ethnographically as well. We thus have a much fuller knowledge of the details of their use, manufacture, or meaning to the culture, as the case may be, than we can ever expect to have of traits known only through archeology. It seems possible that if these traits or trait complexes were to be studied in sufficient detail one might arrive at fairly definite conclusions as to whether they represent independent inventions or are diffused from a single center of origin.

One of the most interesting of these ethnographically-known traits is the manufacture of bark cloth or paper. The technique is known ethno-graphically in South and Middle America, throughout almost all of Oceania and southeast Asia, as well as in tropical portions of Africa. Bark beaters of stone are known archeologically from Middle America and from Indo-nesia, so there can be no question of the antiquity of the trait in these two areas. Now, I think it must be admitted that bark cloth manufacture has, in general, the appearance of something that is not a very obvious thing; it is not a discovery which would be likely to be made more than once, and it has, therefore, been a favorite of those who postulate Asiatic-American contacts. Added to this, it has often been pointed out that bark beaters of stone from Celebes are practically identical to those found archeologically in Mexico.

This situation has intrigued me for a long time, but I recently became especially interested in it when I discovered further that two forms of stone bark beaters are known archeologically in Indonesia, the plain rec-tangular form to which a wooden handle is attached and another where the entire beater, including the handle, is cut from stone, and that both of these types occur in Mesoamerica. This seemed to me to be especially suggestive, and I was able to interest a student in the study of the entire bark cloth complex. The problem posed was that of studying the world-wide distribu-tion of the trait with all its ramifications with the intention of trying to discover whether other elements of the technique bore out the relationships suggested by the similarities in beater form alone. This student has gone far beyond my relatively vague suggestions as to the form this kind of study should take and has found that the seemingly simple trait known as bark cloth manufacture can be broken down into over two hundred dis-tinctive items of beater form, manufacturing procedure, and the uses of bark cloth. Some of these are functionally determined, others not, and their groupings and distributions suggest conclusions of great interest to our problems of Asiatic-American relationships. The full results are unknown to me and in any event I do not wish to anticipate this student's conclu-sions. I have spoken of the study at some length because it illustrates a method of approach which I think is necessary if we are going to investi-gate seriously rather than just debate at a distance the problems of Asiatic-American relationships.

Unfortunately, for the prospect of further studies of this kind, there are relatively few students of ethnography at the present time who can be interested in detailed culture-historical research. If some can be recruited, however, there are other traits which could be handled in a manner similar to the way in which bark cloth manufacture is being treated and could have equally significant results. One which interests me very much is the betel-chewing complex of southeast Asia and the coca-chewing complex of South America. In both cases, lime is added to the principal ingredients and there are suggestions, too, of other related customs which are similar. A detailed study of these practices and of the etiquette, lore, and beliefs connected with them would give some indication of whether or not they are historically related or parallel developments. Another interesting study, but perhaps less promising of significant results, would be a full study of the world distribution of the manufacture and use of blowguns and of the poisons and other equipment used with them. Various of the musical instruments of Asia and the New World, including panpipes, conch shell trumpets, and certain forms of drums have often been thought highly suggestive of trans-Pacific contacts and should be studied intensively, not simply as musical instruments, but in their whole social contexts.

The whole subject of textile manufacture, spinning, loom weaving, and decorating of textiles is an extremely complex subject, but would be well worth intensive study from the point of view of trying to determine whether the American complex is an independent development. Back-strap looms in both world areas are so similar in all their technical details that they are strongly suggestive of relationships, but we will not learn anything about this if there continues to be a strict dichotomy between studies of New World textiles and of Old World textiles.

In every study of the kind I am suggesting, whether of ethnographically known traits or of art motifs, it should logically be as world-wide a study as is possible to make. If occurrences everywhere are not included, one runs the risk of being accused of selecting his materials and of not taking account of other possible developments of the same item or motif. For instance, when I was comparing the lotus panels of India and Mesoamerica, it was pointed out to me that very similar lotus panels are found on the brown-stone houses of New York City constructed in the latter half of the 19th century. As Classic origins were obviously indicated, this led me to look at Classic and even Egyptian design and, although I did not continue to follow the trail, my casual glance at the material suggests that the lotus panels of the early historic periods of India stem originally from elements of Classic design, and that the same source is responsible for those of the "Brownstone Complex."

It is probable, of course, that no one study of the kinds just mentioned concerning the problems of Asiatic-American relationships would be entirely convincing in itself, but I strongly believe that a number of them would give us a perspective toward these problems we certainly do not have at the present time.

There are, to be sure, many other isolated traits and elements which one can suspect of being Asiatically derived. Some may prove to be of considerable importance, but I am not trying here to make as complete a case as possible and I have mentioned only those which seem to offer some prospect of becoming especially meaningful through special research being directed toward them.

Up until now I have been speaking of ways and means of investigating the problems of Asiatic-American relationships, of how we can determine whether there were such relationships, and to what extent they were involved in the origin of the American cultures. As it stands now, I would say that we cannot prove that there were contacts but, on the other hand and just as certainly, I would say that we cannot prove there *were no* important Asiatic-American contacts which would have played an important role in the formation of the American Indian cultures.

I have said nothing about the processes of diffusion, of how the peoples of Asia or Oceania could have come into contact with those of America in a degree sufficient to have transferred to them those ideas we might suspect of having been transferred. I have personally left this for the last because that is where I think it logically belongs. In the past, we have tended to make the mistake of starting with the premise that the Pacific Ocean and sparsely settled shores to the north were all but complete barriers to travel or diffusion and therefore have not found it worth while to investigate further. We cannot, of course, insist too strongly on this point for there would be no problem of Asiatic-American relationships if there were *no possibility* of transfer or diffusion. Actually, it is one of the most difficult aspects of the whole question and not very subject to investigation. The particular events of Pacific crossings or of other movements into America will have to be inferred mainly from the results they produced.

Actual Pacific crossings would be necessary to account for some of our suggested parallels. This implies boats and the ability to navigate long distances. Boats are seldom preserved archeologically, however, and the nature of seafaring practices must remain almost totally unknown when written records do not exist. We can only speculate rather blindly.

In considering the possibilities of early trans-Pacific crossings, several considerations must be kept in mind. We know that extensive navigation in large boats carrying up to two hundred people was common in southeast Asia early in the first millenium A.D., and it is not improbable that boats of this type could have made Pacific crossings either directly across the Pacific or by coasting around the northern route. We probably have to assume contacts of this kind to account for the transfer of the kinds of things we have grouped, for instance, in our Complex A.

There is also the question of travel over long sea distances by smaller craft and here the possibilities are, I feel, often underestimated. In our age of large and comfortable ships, we are inclined to overlook the potentialities of small craft and to underestimate the hardiness of early sailors. The Viking boats were very small, but consider the length and the number of voyages that were made in them. Also, the later peoples of the Pacific were among the world's best in the handling of small craft. It has often been said that the Polynesians who discovered and populated many of the very remote islands of the Pacific would almost certainly have found their way at one time or another to the coasts of America, and I think we would probably all agree that such is very probable. Actually, the presence of the sweet potato in Polynesia constitutes fairly good evidence that contacts across the eastern Pacific did occur and it is hardly logical to think that they did not occur more than once or that the sweet potato is the only cultural transfer that took place as a result of such contacts.

This is very light coverage of the whole and complex subject of early travel in the Pacific, but we cannot go into it more fully here. My feeling is, though, that we cannot blithely use the breadth of the Pacific as a blanket negation of all the suggestive indications that considerable trans-Pacific diffusion did occur.

The other diffusional route from Asia into the New World is by land through the Bering Straits region, and we find an ever-increasing number of North American specialists who are becoming fairly convinced that Woodland-type pottery, burial mounds, and a number of specific artifact types found in their area might stem originally from northeast Asia. At the same time, radiocarbon determinations have tended to push back the dating of the earliest of these cultures in North America to a point where it is almost possible to conceive of them as marking the route of the introduction of the pottery-making idea into the New World as a whole. Is it possible, in other words, that North America saw the introduction of pottery and agriculture at a remote time and that these ideas were taken up and speedily developed in Middle America or in regions further south? This may not be as fantastic as it sounds. It would depend for substantiation on the finding of some such evidence as fabric-marked or other similarly surfaced wares in the earliest periods in the Mesoamerican area and there are some hints that such might occur. Furthermore, our rapidly developing knowledge of the archeology of northwestern North America might supply relevant information.

One wonders, furthermore, to what extent the Bering Straits route may have served for the quick passage of small groups of people and the transfer of important culture ideas from Asia to America for which we could not expect to find a legible archeological record. Speculation along these lines must be kept within bounds, but I suspect that primitive and semi-civilized people traveled a great deal more, and at least knew more of far distant peoples and cultures, than is usually thought. The archeological record is nearly always so fragmentary and such a poor reflection of the total culture that indications of this are not often included in what we can get from that record. Our historic and ethnographic knowledge of most groups is also based upon material gathered during periods when the presence of Europeans had already brought the relationships of neighboring groups into imbalance so that we do not have a true picture of what such relationships were before that major disturbance occurred.

I would question, therefore, whether individuals or small groups of people may not have traveled from China, let us say, well into North America or even further south in a matter of ten or twenty years and have been responsible for the introduction of new ideas. The record of some of the early European travelers in the Americas—such as Cabeza de Vaca, who wandered through primitive tribes across Texas and northern Mexico without being killed, or the early fur traders, who easily found their way far into the interior of North America through several tribal groups—is some indication that such travel was not impossible. Generally speaking, too, in the areas of more advanced cultures and larger political units there would be relatively less suspicion of foreigners and a higher receptivity to foreign ideas.

In effect, I am postulating for this northern area a kind of stimulus diffusion brought about most likely by traveling bands but also to a certain extent perhaps by the passage of knowledge of novel ways of life from group to group. By this means, there could be a diffusion of ideas from one area of high culture to another—from China to Mesoamerica—without leaving any trace which could necessarily be detected archeologically in the area of its passage. I do not see that we have to have a continuous areal distribution—either archeologically or ethnographically determined—of any particular trait before we can suspect its dispersal from one area to another.

Some of the suggestions I have just made would apply also to trans-Pacific contacts established by boat travel. It has often been suspected, I believe, that landings established by Pacific or Asiatic peoples on the shores of America would not be effective because the occupants of the boats would be either immediately killed or the newcomers, greatly outnumbered, could have no effect on the local cultures. These I feel are entirely unwarranted assumptions. Generalizations cannot be made as to what would happen in these kinds of meetings without taking into consideration the nature of the cultures involved and of the particulars of the encounters. I would guess, for instance, that a large junk-like boat from Indonesia landing on the Pacific coast of Mexico in the 8th century A.D. would probably meet with a favorable reception not unlike that afforded Cortez at Vera Cruz in the 16th century. If there were Buddhist priests on board they could conceivably have been well received by the upper classes of the highly stratified society of some important ceremonial center. I think it possible, too, that they eventually could have had a fairly noticeable effect on religious customs or the religious art of this center.

These are rather wild speculations, perhaps, on the manner in which Asiatic-American relationship could have come about, and at the moment they are far from being subject to verification. They seem to be necessary, however, as a beginning toward some discussion of the means and processes that would be involved in Asiatic-American contacts or relationships. Perhaps, with proper studies we can prove that such contacts occurred, or perhaps someday we will find a figure of Buddha at Palenque or a late Chou bronze at Tajín and then we will have to find some means of getting it there. Most likely, however, both portions of the story, indications of relationship and knowledge of how it could have come about, will be developed slowly and simultaneously and we will wake up some day to find that we have explained the whole history of how the cultures of the Old World influenced those of the New World—if there is anything to this at all.

LINGUISTICS AND THE RECONSTRUCTION OF CULTURE HISTORY

George L. Trager

MORE THAN A THIRD of a century ago, Edward Sapir wrote his *Time Perspective in Aboriginal American Culture, a Study in Method* (1916). In it he gave us all the important points to be kept in mind in establishing time depth in culture history, and showed what linguistics can contribute. Sapir's paper has been read and reread by all today's anthropologists, but its precepts and cautions are still largely unheeded. We shall try to show here, in the light of some of the more recent developments in linguistics and in culture theory, how important it is to evaluate properly the linguistic contribution to culture history if we seek to arrive at the over-all history of cultures.

Some general notions must be established first. In the Western cultures, history has always been a preoccupation. To us time is measurable, and measured, and no situation makes sense until it has been located in time. Having done that, we then proceed to explain that which comes after by what has come before. Modern science, no matter how culture-free it seeks to become, is a product of Western culture. Every field of science is thus historical-minded. Astronomers seek to establish relative and absolute chronologies for the whole universe. Biologists investigate evolutionary processes. The sciences of culture seek origins and sequences to explain the present.

Thus archeology has always attracted the attention even of laymen, for it uncovers the past. Ethnology that deals with "primitives" also seems to be pointing to evolutionary processes, and comparative philology is almost the only aspect of linguistic science that the non-specialist has heard about or shows any interest in.

Whatever the culturologist's impatience to get to history, he has learned nonetheless that he must toil away at synchronic description first. It is here that the linguist comes most forcefully into the picture, for the descriptive structural linguist has perforce come to have an understanding of history that is different from the superficial approach possible where only limited data exist. The linguist has learned that his aspect of culture—language— is a complex system that can be described at any point in time. He knows that even synchronically it is not static, but that every event that takes place in the system is an event in time—a historical happening. He thus learns that the better and more detailed his descriptions of structural inter-relations, and the more points in time for which he has such descriptions, the more accurate and penetrating does his history become.

The linguist, then, points out how language is structured and suggests that that structure is a model for the analysis of other cultural systems. He then shows how he establishes historical relationships and developmental sequences, arguing that similar procedures will work in every cultural field. He points out, in the end, that by tying up structural sequences in many fields, the overall culturologist may some day establish convincing absolute chronologies.

The comparative linguistics of the 19th century, with its sound-laws without exceptions and its seemingly rigid family-trees of linguistic relationship, appeared to the non-linguist student of culture to have achieved something that he himself could never attain. Now, although we know that the "sound-laws" are merely statements summarizing prevailing sequences of change and that the family-trees are at best schemes of relative chronological relationship, it is still true that the detailed and exact comparisons that are possible in linguistics seem somehow to offer no fruitful leads in other fields of culture. An examination of what it is exactly that the historical linguist does, will show why this is.

When it is suspected that two languages, say Taos and Kiowa, or French and Italian, are related, the linguist (ideally) makes full and explicit statements of the phonemic and morphological systems of the two languages, and lists their morphemes in *extenso* (as words or as stems, and as affixes). He then makes point-by-point comparisons. Thus French /s/ in *six* is found to correspond to Italian /s/ in *sei*, but the /š/ of *cinq* corresponds to Italian /č/ in *cinque*; French /š/ in *champ* corresponds to Italian /k/ in *campo*, French /k/ in *coeur* to /k/ in *cuore*, /k/ in *quand* to /kw/ in *quando*. The French verb forms *savoir, su, sache* correspond, sound by sound, and in stems and suffixes, to Italian *sapere, saputo, sappia*. French vocabulary items like *tête, corps, mère, pied* (and so on, by the thousands) correspond to Italian *testa, corpo, madre, pie*. In similar fashion, Taos and Kiowa can be compared (typographical difficulties require this statement to be taken on faith here).

The comparisons having been made, reconstruction is then attempted. French /s/ and Italian /s/ are taken to be unchanged reflexes of Latin /s/

in *sex;* /s/ and /č/ are taken back to an original palatal stop, so that we know that Latin *quinque* must have become **k̑inque* before giving the French and Italian forms; /š/ and /k/ are assumed to go back to /k/ in *campus;* /k/ and /k/ to /k/ in *cor,* /k/ and /kw/ to /kw/ in *quando.* The verb forms cited go back to *sapere, saputum* (a form not known in Classical Latin) and *sapiam.* The vocabulary items listed testify to Latin *testa* (meaning "pot" and not "head"!), *corpus, matrem, pedem.*

From the reconstructions emerges a Proto-Romanic, a language not attested except sporadically in so-called errors in inscriptions and ancient documents; but we happen to possess many attestations of Latin and thus know that our reconstructions are correct, and that Proto-Romanic is the form of spoken Latin that resulted in the modern Romanic languages. If we were comparing Taos and Kiowa, we would arrive at a reconstructed Tano-Kiowan (Trager, 1951). For this language we have no direct supporting evidence in written form. The techniques of reconstruction, however, have been so widely tested that we know they are reliable; and the possibility of reconstructing a Proto-Uto-Aztecan, and then an Azteco-Tanoan, provides another kind of support in terms of mutual consistency.

The linguist is able to make the kinds of statements alluded to in the preceding section because he knows that every language is organized along the same lines. He knows that the basic units are phonemes and morphemes, and that these are used in constructions (words, clauses, sentences) that constitute a system of reference to the rest of the culture of the group speaking the language. Linguistics has made great strides in the analysis of phonological and morphological structures, but is still unable to handle the reference-level, which might be called semology. However, we do know that linguistic forms have meaning and we use vocabulary items as clues to these meanings. Presumably, to have become the word for "head" in French and Italian, Latin *testa* must have been not only the word for "pot" but also must have been used as a slang term for "head." This tells us about Latin vocabulary and also implies something about Latin humor—at the least.

Not only is vocabulary used as indicated, but it has recently been suggested that by comparing 'vocabularies we can arrive at rather exact measures of the chronological distance between them. Some go even further and say this gives us exact measurements for the dates of separation of two languages; it would be strange, indeed, if this were so, since languages consist of much more than vocabulary. But in any case, linguistic data can be used as the basis for several kinds of rather precise conclusions as to point-by-point phonemic and morphemic relationship, relative chronology, and possibly absolute chronology of some kind.

The ethnologist has available to him the kind of contemporary data that the linguist has, and here and there in the world he can find historical records full enough to be anthropologically useful. Moreover, he has the archeologist to show him the material remains of culture. Why then does he not reconstruct the past with the precision of the linguist?

The answer seems simple. No one has yet established, except in a few small areas of culture such as kinship and some aspects of technology, any-thing like the basic analysis into phonological and morphological entities that linguists use. The ethnologist—the culturologist in general—needs to work on his theory until he is able to separate out the hundreds of cultural systems (analogous to language) that exist—systems of social grouping, relationship, class, status, family structure, time measurement, magic, arti-faction, and so on. For each system—delimited so that it is seen to deal with events of the same order—he must establish the basic isolates, sets, and patterns. The isolates must be units analogous—at that level—to pho-nemes, the sets to morphemes, the patterns to the as yet unanalyzed refer-ence-units.[1]

When there exist analytical schemes for describing, say, government organization in terms of its isolates and sets (and patterns), then we can apply such schemes to describing the government structure of the Taos and Kiowa, and can perhaps (probably?) discover that these are *not* related, although the two languages are rather closely related. Without any over-all scheme of this kind, but because of the handleable nature of the data, something of this sort can be done for kinship systems already. In the case of Taos and Kiowa, the two are seen to be wholly different in their kinship systems, so that no vocabulary resemblance exists in this part of the language.

Similarly, archeologists can now compare details of some kinds of artifacts—pottery types, arrowheads—and come to conclusions as to rela-tionships and historical origin. The relationships thus established often show no parallel to those existing linguistically. This, of course, is as it should be. Every cultural system and subsystem must be analyzed in and of itself, and its historical connections established in their own terms.

After a good many comparative treatments in different fields exist, then one can attempt to bring them together and arrive at further con-clusions. Let us imagine, at some distant future, the existence of good "grammars" of not only the Taos language but also the kinship system, government organization, patterns of man-woman relationships, systems of orientation in space and time, enculturation techniques, recreational sys-tems, ritual, organization of military defense, house-building techniques,

---

[1] For a preliminary version of such an over-all analytical scheme, see Hall and Trager, 1953.

boot and moccasin making, corn planting (to list but a few). In each of these descriptions, we will be shown the basic units at various levels and how they are combined in patterns; the structure will be made clear, and we will have something more than a mass of isolated and unrelated details. Then let us further imagine a corresponding set of such "grammars" for Kiowa. The items of the two sets can then be compared one by one: we know that the languages will be seen to be systematically related; we can surmise that some of the other systems will also show relationship, while others will be wholly unlike. For the latter, we will seek relationship else-where. Eventually, we will be able to construct a series of interlocking chronologies which will show an over-all pattern. Then we can say, per-haps, that Taos and Kiowa are groups that separated linguistically 1000 to 1500 years ago, that one or the other (or both) replaced an original kin-ship system of one kind by systems of another type at such and such a date, that the Taos got their pottery, such as it was, from such a source at such a time while the Kiowa never had pottery, and so on.

Archeologists and culture-historians, in general, on being confronted with the kind of program outlined above are likely to react with disap-pointment to its difficulties or to dismiss it as fantasy. For it will be pointed out that there are areas where chronology is rather definitely estab-lished and where available dates from different sources agree well enough with each other. Why, then, wait for elaborate analytical schemes when short-cuts to history seem to exist already.

First, let us point out that even if history is an end in itself, it is not a sole end. There have been many occasions in the history of the West-ern and other literate cultures when history has been rewritten for political and other immediate purposes. If it is possible to revise interpretations of written history, how much more subject to revision must the history be which is based upon interpretation of artifacts, radiocarbon decay, tree-ring growth, or vocabulary attrition.

Second, it is necessary to remember that it has always been a tenet of anthropological science that race, language, and "culture" are indepen-dent of each other, and not necessarily affected by each other. Putting any discussion of race aside as irrelevant here, and reiterating our belief that "culture" not only includes language but is itself not one thing but a com-plex of many systems, we can emphasize that if this is so the various cul-tural systems, including language, must necessarily be considered as having the possibility of evolving and changing independently. When a group of people split into two groups, we may say that from that moment there are two societies with two languages and two over-all cultures; for since the people who talk and otherwise interact with each other are no longer the same, there is, inevitably, some change in what is said and done. But the structures and even the details of the languages or of any other cultural systems may remain almost the same for long periods. Moreover, the vocabulary may shift quite independently of anything else, or the artifacts may change but the old vocabulary continue in use.

If it is argued that the recently proposed "glottochronology" techniques have value, it must first be established what that value is. The measurement deals with change in a "basic" vocabulary. If the vocabulary is really "non-cultural" and adequate, the fact still remains that *all* that can be measured by it is extent of vocabulary change. Language structure, language relationship, the ties between the language and the rest of the culture—all these *are not* and *cannot* be measured by vocabulary counts. As pointed out above, the Taos and Kiowa languages are sufficiently alike structurally and in much of their vocabulary to enable us to reconstruct (with the aid of data from other Tanoan languages) a Proto-Tano-Kiowan, say about 1500 years ago. A confirmation of this date by glottochronology would give no indication one way or another of the very close resemblance in phonological and grammatical detail of the two languages. Nor would it show, or even reflect, the otherwise vast differences in the culture of the two groups. Likewise, the dating by radiocarbon or by dendrochronology of artifacts now associated with the Taos or the Kiowa can in no way indicate that the persons who made the artifacts spoke one or another of these languages or some ancestral form of either or both.

It has been said many times that you can't add horses and apples. Similarly, in culture history you can't tie in vocabulary change with a dated piece of pottery or wooden artifact. The vocabulary must be situated in its own cultural system—the language. The artifacts must be situated in their respective cultural systems. When and if the various systems are independently analyzed historically, then—and only then—can developmental patterns be compared and over-all historical tie-ins recognized. Otherwise we have only misleading and facile leaping to conclusions.

THE COMING OF AGE OF AMERICAN ARCHEOLOGY

Betty J. Meggers

THE PAPERS in this volume provide us with interpretative summaries of the status of archeological research in a number of New World areas. Many of the ideas put forth are new and exciting; some would have been inconceivable a decade ago and even now are revolutionary in their effect on our traditional view of cultural development in the Americas. Some readers, I am sure, have been able to accept the majority of these conclusions. Others have probably rejected the same reconstructions of the development and diffusion of culture on the ground that they are unscientifically derived or at least lacking in sufficient proof. Between these is a third type of reader, who probably represents the majority opinion. He is uncertain because, although he is stimulated by the apparent reasonableness and simplicity of these explanations of cultural development, he remembers the discredited evolutionary and diffusional theories of the past and cannot overcome the reservation that these archeologists have been led into similar errors.

The important question is, therefore, are the new ideas and interpretations "scientific"? One thing we can be sure of: to dismiss Ekholm's trans-Pacific influence, Spaulding's Mexican origin for Adena and Middle Mississippi traits, or any of the other reconstructions of past events as merely prejudice on the part of the writer would indeed be unscientific. Because this question must be answered before we can accept or reject the interpretations on their own merits, it will be appropriate to examine briefly those sciences we consider to be models of the scientific approach—the physical sciences—to see how the procedures and assumptions employed by these archeologists rate as examples of scientific method.

If we look at the papers together rather than as separate, distinct contributions, it is readily apparent that most of the authors have made use of the same basic cultural principles and have drawn similar general conclusions from them. One of these is the principle that the existence of a complex trait or group of traits in two geographically separated regions cannot be the result of independent development, but must be attributed to cultural contact. Whether this is diffusion of culture or migration of people,

116

we are accustomed to visualize it as a typically slow and gradual process. However, one striking conclusion reached by several writers is the speed with which cultural traits spread in a number of instances in the Americas. Willey is the only one who can support his conclusion by actual dates derived from Carbon 14, but it is implicit in the reconstructions made by Evans and Spaulding. Willey was able to demonstrate that certain non-contemporary traits, among them rocker stamping, platform mounds, negative painting, and mold-made figurines, appear at almost the same time in Mexico and Peru and must in each case be considered to have diffused from a single origin. Since there is little prospect of discovering a geographically intermediate source of diffusion, this represents a rapid movement of traits that have no apparent practical value to explain their swift spread. Similarly, Eiseley sees the expansion of the human race to the ends of the earth as something that occurred, as he so graphically phrased it, "in the blink of a geological eye."

Rapid movements of whole complexes that seem to require the assumption of migration of peoples were postulated by Evans for northern South America and by Spaulding for eastern North America. These share with Ekholm's conclusions on the origin of certain Mesoamerican cultures the feature of absence of evidence as yet along the presumed route of transmittal and, what is more striking, absence of an as yet defined ancestral complex in the presumed place of origin. Evans traces the Marajoara culture at the mouth of the Amazon, an intrusive culture with close Circum-Caribbean and Sub-Andean affiliations, to the northwestern corner of South America but correspondences in that part of the continent are scattered and general in our present state of knowledge. Spaulding, in a similar way, derives the Adena culture of the Ohio Valley from northeastern Mexico but acknowledges that a predecessor in that region has not yet been found. Ekholm faces the same problem in his attempts to find a specific derivation for the elements of Asiatic appearance in Mesoamerica. When Spaulding and Evans make these reconstructions, we remember the terrestrial links and are prone to accept the conclusion that contact took place, but when the sea intervenes, as it does in Ekholm's case, we are more resistant. It is well to keep in mind, however, that these three individuals are drawing on the same type of evidence and if detailed resemblances preclude the possibility of independent invention, as we usually agree that they do, then the transmittal must have occurred whether we can visualize the method or not.

Another cultural principle that has been drawn upon by several of our writers is environmental determinism. Eiseley visualizes an Old World Paleolithic culture adapted to the hunting of large game, which was funneled through or dispersed over grasslands that occupied large areas of the earth's surface in glacial and early post-glacial times. As this world environment gave way to diverse local conditions, cultures became locally specialized, producing the differences represented archeologically by Paleo-Indian and Archaic complexes in the Americas. Spaulding resorted to environmental explanations several times in assessing the possibilities of cultural diffusion into the eastern United States from Asia and from the boreal zone of North America. Evans discussed it in greater detail as it explains the absence of archeological evidence to support Steward's hypothesis that the Tropical Forest type of culture developed in the Guianas and spread from there throughout the Tropical Forest Area.

A third important principle employed by several writers is cultural evolution. Both Evans and Spaulding express cultural differences in terms of stages or levels of development and both relate these levels to subsistence resources, with a well-developed social organization, elaborate arts and crafts, funerary practices, and earthworks dependent upon a productive agricultural economy. Willey utilizes such terms as "Formative" and "Early Classic" to refer to comparable stages of development in Mexico, Yucatan, Central America, and the Andean Area of South America, and Reed notes the increasing acceptance of this type of evolutionary framework in the American Southwest.

If we are to accept any or all of these "new interpretations of American culture history," we must be prepared to accept the assumptions or principles upon which they are based. This includes some form of evolutionary development of culture, some form of environmental determinism, and the recognition that detailed cultural resemblances are evidence of cultural diffusion whatever the obstacles to its occurrence appear to have been. All of these are old ideas in anthropology, all have been enthusiastically espoused and vehemently denied. Our problem is to decide whether they are scientific theories that can be accepted as working tools, or whether they are products of distortion and ignorance of the facts and, therefore, misleading if not useless.

In order to do this, we must find a satisfactory method of determining what is "scientific." The achievements of the physicists have built up for us, as for other laymen, the image of "Science" with a capital S. This "Science" is composed of two parts carefully controlled experiments, one part meticulous measurement, and three parts complex mathematical equations or formulae. Before this spectacle, some anthropologists have stepped back in awe and declared that "social science" can never be "real science." Others have praised Boas for his "rigorous methodology" and devoted themselves to following his lead in substituting fact gathering and the solution

of specific local problems for "armchair theorizing" and "premature generalization." The latest effort to draw the mantle of Science over anthropology appears to be inspired by the fact that mathematics is one of the
more obvious ingredients in modern physics. The pressure to make it also an
ingredient of anthropology impinges upon us constantly. In fact, we can
hardly open a recent copy of any of our journals without finding an article
admonishing us to retreat from the swamps now supporting our shaky conclusions to the firmer ground of statistical tests and demonstrations. While
we can protest that the application of statistical formulae gives no new
or better results, this answer gives us no assurance that to operate without
mathematical proof is a scientific procedure. What we really need to know
is, what is "scientific analysis."

When we think of physics, one of the first associations we make is
with scientific laws. Physics means the law of gravitation, the laws of
motion, the laws of thermodynamics, etc. We think of these as the basic
rules obeyed by the atoms and the stars, immutable, inescapable, and eter-
nal, and our reaction is that anthropology can never achieve anything like
this. If we investigate further, however, we find the physicists eager to
explain that many of their laws are not a description of a process followed
invariably and uniformly by each and every atom but instead are a statistical
average. An example is the law of mechanics, which states that there is an
increase in molecular motion with the rise of temperature and that this
increase proceeds at an even rate. This law does not apply to each individual
particle in a mixture, however, because the heavier ones always move
more slowly than the lighter ones. The proposition is only statistically true,
as at any given moment any given molecule may be traveling at an extraordinarily great velocity or may be almost motionless. The majority, however, would be close to the average value and this average value is the
same for molecules of any substance at any given temperature (Gamow,
1945, pp. 24-26). There are two possible reasons for our ready acceptance
of such statistical laws in physics and our resistance to accepting them
in the social sciences: First, we cannot see the exceptions when they are
atoms or molecules and it is easy to forget that they exist; and Second, we
are not accustomed to explaining the actions of deviant atoms or molecules
as motivated by choice. In the social sciences, the deviant particles are
human beings with individual personalities, whom we find it inhumane to
reduce to the level of a statistic.

Even in those situations where the deviant particle is a culture or a
tribe, we resist the application of a statistical approach to generalization.
This is evident in the opposition to the concept of environmental influence
on culture. While the proponents of this view have variously insisted that

119

a culture is determined by its environment or that it is at least limited in certain ways by its environment (as in the example that snow houses cannot be used where there is no snow), its opponents have pointed out that similar cultures exist in very different geographical settings and that any systematic connection between environment and culture is thus obviously refuted.

However, the more we learn about the basis of cultural development, and especially the significance of the subsistence pattern, the clearer it becomes that environment does have an important influence upon cultural development through the differential potentiality it has for subsistence exploitation. By and large, environments that do not permit agriculture limit the cultural adjustment to a far lower level than those where agriculture can be employed. There are also differences in the intensity of agricultural production that can be achieved in different climates and soils, which in turn influence the cultural adjustment. This is not a uniform or invariable correlation, but it can be shown that hunting and gathering groups exist where the environment prohibits agriculture and that, while they differ in details of their culture and even in degree of primitiveness, on the average they are nomadic, their material culture is simple, their social organization is on the family level, and their religious concepts are vague. Other types of environments with different subsistence resources are associated with other general types or levels of culture, forming a continuous sequence that culminates in our own civilization (cf. Meggers, 1954).

If we think back a moment to the physicists' statistical law of mechanics, it will be noted that the kind of association anthropologists make between environment and culture is similar to that made by the physicists between temperature and molecular motion. Their law says, when the temperature rises, the molecules move faster *on the average*. Our law says, as the environment improves in subsistence potential, the culture advances in complexity, *on the average*. Once the physicists recognized their law of mechanics, they went on to discover that the deviant particles also obeyed a law and this discovery has had an important application to the problems of the liberation of sub-atomic energy (Gamow, 1945, p. 28). Since such statistical laws work so well for physicists, there is no reason why anthropologists should not give them a try. There is everything to gain, since such an approach not only permits prediction but also suggests new avenues for investigation.

Some laws of physics are not averages but are statements of the reaction that will always occur in a given situation, other things being equal. "Other things being equal" is the stereotyped way of saying that disturbing factors are not present to influence or alter the expected outcome. In the case of the first law of motion, however, other things are never equal. This law states that the natural motion of a body is motion at a uniform speed in a straight line. Nowhere in the universe can this be observed; it is something of which we have no experience for, if all other disturbing factors are removed, gravitation is always present to distort the motion. In justification of reliance on such a law, one scientist says:

"Why, then, did scientific men choose, as the foundation for their reasoning about motion, a law that can never be verified by observation? They chose the law because it was the most convenient possible law to choose. It introduced an unrivalled simplicity and economy into the complicated phenomena of motion. . . . It describes an unobservable state of affairs, but all observable states of affairs can be accounted for much more simply if we assume it . . . The first law describes what would happen if there were no disturbing forces, and the fact that what it describes never does happen is explained by the fact that there always are disturbing forces" (Sullivan, 1933, pp. 58-59).

If we turn back for a moment to the theories of anthropology, we are immediately struck by the resemblance between this approach and the criticisms that have been directed at the law of cultural evolution: that few if any tribes have passed through the stages of development described, that this possibility is actually obviated by the universal presence of diffusion, and that to divorce culture from its specific occurrences and to describe it as if it had a vitality of its own is unwarranted. On these objections, the theory of cultural evolution has not only been denied the status of a law but has been labeled as a false, misleading, indefensible, and even ridiculous doctrine.

The above discussion of the first law of motion, however, indicates that a scientific law need not describe any observable condition. Its validity stems from the fact that observable conditions can be more easily understood and more simply explained if the law is assumed. An increasing number of anthropologists, and particularly archeologists, are beginning to recognize this advantage in the law of cultural evolution. Willey, Strong, Bennett, and Armillas have profitably used the concept of developmental stages in analyzing the archeological sequences of Peru and Mexico (Kroeber, 1948a, pp. 114 and 116). Childe (1951) has clearly stated the same kind of approach to the prehistory of Europe, and Steward (1949b) has attempted to show that all of the ancient high cultures of the world followed a similar evolutionary pattern of development. Thus, although cultural evolution is often denied in the abstract today, it is being relied upon with increasing frequency as a research tool because of the fact that, as with the first law of motion, "all observable states of affairs can be accounted for much more simply if we assume it."

There is a third category of physical laws that is purely descriptive. An example is Kepler's laws of planetary motion: that the planets move in elliptical orbits, that their velocity increases as they approach the sun, and that they move more slowly the farther their orbits are from the sun. These laws are statements of fact and describe an observable situation with no exceptions. We might equate this kind of law with a third basic assumption employed in these papers, namely, that a complex composed of a number of distinctive elements or traits can originate only once, and that all occurrences must, therefore, be related. Numerous diffusion studies have provided evidence for this belief and it appears to qualify as a descriptive law, although it has been objected that man is not so uninventive that it is necessary to fall back on such a conclusion.

If we concede, for the moment, that our anthropological principles have the same outward form as some of the laws in physics, we may go on to examine what the physicists require in the way of proof for their laws. There is a possibility that our cultural "laws" may have the form but lack the substance. In anthropology, the burden of proof usually rests with the person who bases his conclusions on the terms of a generalization rather than on the person who questions these conclusions. In the case of trans-Pacific diffusion, the basic postulate that two identical or nearly-identical complexes cannot arise independently is rarely attacked. Instead, unanswerable questions are raised such as: "If this is so, why did not the wheel diffuse also?" Or, in the case of Andean-Mesoamerican relationships, "Why was writing not adopted by the Peruvians?"

Such objections, of course, get us nowhere because they lead into the realm of pure speculation. For each of these questions we can think of an answer, but the answers are irrelevant to the facts and can bring us no progress in the understanding of cultural processes. It is a measure of the immaturity of our science that we insist upon asking ourselves why certain things did not occur instead of trying to understand first why things happened as they did. The physicists have long since abandoned this dead-end approach, having learned that when they were able to explain what did happen they could also generally explain what did not. What ignorance suggests to be equally possible alternatives often turn out in reality not to be so at all.

That we still fall into these errors is also partly a result of the intimacy with which we are related to our subject matter. A modern physicist is under no obligation to reduce the behavior of the stars and planets to rational explanations in terms of human personality, as did his astrologist predecessor. However, we still preserve this approach to the explanation of past human events. As if anthropocentrism by itself were not a sufficient mistake, we tend to take the point of view of twentieth century American culture, thereby violating one of our cardinal principles—that objectivity is inconsistent with ethnocentrism. Once we divorce ourselves from such notions as that writing and the wheel are the foundation of civilization, and recognize the fact that advanced civilizations have existed in the absence of both, we will be better able to formulate for ourselves questions whose answers can be found.

If we should come to a conclusion about the operation of culture, how are we to determine its validity? It is somewhat disappointing, at first, to learn that the most eminent physicists assert that proof of a scientific hypothesis is impossible. Jeans, for instance, states:

"In real science . . . a hypothesis can never be proved true. If it is negatived by future observations we shall know it is wrong but if future observations confirm it we shall never be able to say it is right, since it will always be at the mercy of still further observations" (1943, p. 181).

Eddington speaks in a similar vein:

"We cannot pretend to offer proofs. *Proof* is an idol before whom the pure mathematician tortures himself. In physics we are generally content to sacrifice before the lesser shrine of *Plausibility*" (1928, p. 337).

Einstein also has been quoted as saying, "No amount of experimentation can ever prove me right; a single experiment may at any time prove me wrong" (Heyl, 1954, p. 274).

Although it may be shocking at first to hear the physicists themselves state in such uncompromising terms that their laws are not the hard and fast, tried and true, tested and proved, permanent and immutable formulations that we have conceived them to be, it is of the greatest significance to us that such is the case. It changes the whole situation in regard to the possibility of arriving at generalizations or laws in the realm of cultural phenomena. If the laws of physics are as the physicists themselves describe them, then some of the objections that are offered against cultural laws— that they are not proved, or that they may turn out to have exceptions— lose their force.

If proof is not possible, what are the criteria that are used to judge the relative validity of two physical theories? If we set aside the cases where a theory was abandoned because it failed to account for a newly observed situation, in other words, where it was disproved, we find that

123

one criterion of truth keeps reappearing in the writings of physicists. As Jeans puts it:

"When two hypotheses are possible, we provisionally choose that which our minds adjudge to be the simpler, on the supposition that this is the more likely to lead in the direction of the truth" (1943, p. 183).

A striking example of the application of this criterion exists in the history of astronomy. About 140 A.D., Ptolemy of Alexandria outlined a scheme of the universe based on the principle that the earth was its fixed center. He put forth strong arguments against the possibility of the earth's moving, including the conclusion that if it did the air would be left behind and the flying birds could not keep up. Although these "proofs" sound ridiculous to us today, they convinced the best scholars for more than a thousand years. It was not until Copernicus' work was published in 1546 that an alternative hypothesis was proposed, in which the earth and the other planets were asserted to revolve about the sun. Although Copernicus could offer no real proof for his conclusion, and was able in the last analysis to point only to the greater simplicity of his theory as its major advantage over Ptolemy's this was sufficient to gain it a foothold in scientific thought (Reichenbach, 1942, p. 18). It was only when Newton came along more than a hundred years later that the first real demonstration that Copernicus was correct was advanced.

In explaining why Newton's first law of motion—that the natural motion of a body is in a straight line at a uniform speed—has been adopted by physicists as the cornerstone of reasoning about motion in spite of the fact that such motion can never be observed, Sullivan falls back on this same virtue of simplicity:

"They chose the law because it was the most convenient law to choose. It introduced unrivalled simplicity and economy into the complicated phe-nomena of motion. For it must be remembered that what scientific men mean by truth is, in the last resort, convenience" (1933, pp. 58-59).

Jeans has remarked that in our search for truth,

"Apart from our knowledge of the patterns of events, our tools can only be probable reasoning and the principle of simplicity" (1943, p. 190).

And finally, Dirac, who won the Nobel Prize for Physics in 1933, says:

"With all the violent changes to which physical theory is subjected in modern times, there is just one rock which weathers every storm, to which one can always hold fast—the assumption that the fundamental laws of nature correspond to a beautiful mathematical theory. This means a theory based on simple mathematical concepts that fit together in an elegant way, so that one has pleasure in working with it. So when a theoretical physicist has found such a theory, people put great confidence in it. If a discrepancy should turn up between the predictions of such a theory and an experimental result, one's first reaction would be to suspect experimental error, and only after exhaustive experimental checks would one accept the view that the theory needs modification, which would mean that one must look for a theory with a still more beautiful mathematical basis" (1954, p. 143).

Note the criteria that are emphasized here—simplicity, convenience, beauty—and compare them with the oft-repeated terms of derogation used in anthropology and the bitterness with which "simpliste" explanations and efforts to reduce the infinitely variable and complex individual expressions of culture to their fundamental generalities have been assailed. Whereas a simple theory is considered the highest ideal in physics, in anthropology it is decried as suspect or branded as useless.

Since one of the arguments brought up with considerable frequency to refute cultural interpretations is that they violate the "dictates of common sense" (Herskovits, 1948, p. 512; Dixon, 1928, pp. 189-190 and 265-6), it might be well to see what the physicists think of this criterion of truth. We have all heard of Einstein's theory of relativity but most of us know little of it beyond the name. There is one interesting situation deriving from this theory that is pertinent here, and that is the conclusion that movement exercises a retarding influence on clocks. If two clocks register the same time and one is moved about while the other remains stationary, the moving clock will be slower than its stationary counterpart when it is finally returned to its original position. This effect is produced in all running mechanisms, including the physical-chemical changes in the human body, since all are based on atoms. Furthermore, the faster the movement, the greater is the retardation. In the realm of ordinary experience, this situation has little significance. However, when the speed approaches that of light and is maintained over great distances, striking implications develop. Such a situation will arise if we ever succeed in developing interplanetary travel. Our space ship will cover astronomical distances at speeds approaching that of light. According to the theory of relativity, the human passengers on this flight will have their bodily processes slowed down, so that they will age more slowly than they would normally. If they returned to earth after an absence of several decades, they would look and feel only slightly older than when they departed, but they would find that others of their generation who had remained behind were aged or already dead. This conclusion sounds incredible, so let us turn to an authority for justification. Reichenbach says:

"This example has caused much surprise and even controversy in the discussion of the theory of relativity; but it is impossible to deny that it follows necessarily from the theory of relativity and that all physical facts speak for the correctness of the contention. The theory of relativity will not declare, to be sure, anything concerning the possibility of ever traveling across the space of the universe, for the simple reason that prophesies with regard to technical progress are outside its domain. But it may assert that, if such a trip is undertaken, the travelers are bound to age slower. . . . The hypothetical form of the assertion is right, even compulsory, insofar as all available facts are in favor of the doctrine of relativity. We cannot accept the objection that the case is inconceivable. Quite the contrary, everything described in it is quite conceivable; and fiction has more than once restored to such imagery. . . . The novelty of the case consists only in that it is now the imagery which represents the truth" (1942, pp. 69-70).

I am sure that few of us would presume to question these assertions. Our faith in modern physics is such that however fantastic the conclusions seem, we marvel but believe. Why is it, then, that when it is suggested that men may have crossed the Pacific in boats a few centuries before Columbus traversed the Atlantic, we protest that our credulity is being overstrained and insist that absolute proof be adduced not only that this could have been done but that it actually was done? Why do we resist the lesser marvel while we accept the truly incredible? We would do well to give this paradox serious thought, and to ask ourselves whether our resistance really has a scientific basis. The absence of striking advances in non-mathematical sciences comparable to those in physics has not escaped notice by other scientists, and one physicist has commented that "it may be through the limitations of common sense that these sciences are in their relatively unsatisfactory condition" (Sullivan, 1933, p. 282).

There is one final point on which we might profitably examine the attitude of the physicists and this concerns the way in which scientific theories are derived. With the sharp criticisms directed against the cultural theorists of the past still ringing in our ears, we have generally concerned ourselves with sticking close to the facts and proposing conclusions only when they seem to be proved beyond the possibility of contradiction. We tend to feel that when the data are complete, the conclusion will be self-evident, like a ripe fruit that only needs plucking from the tree. However, the physicists think differently. Einstein has said:

"We now realize, with special clarity, how much in error are those theorists who believe that theory comes inductively from experience (1950, p. 72).

Sullivan goes even further to say:

"The present-day difficulties of physics itself probably spring from the fact that its imaginative efforts have not been imaginative enough. We are still hampered by our habitual modes of thought even when, as with the

126

modern mathematical physicist, they have departed a long way from common sense" (1933, p. 282).

The problem of training imaginative researchers has become a matter
of deep concern in physics, and is one of the major points made in a recent
address by R. E. Gibson, Director of the Applied Physics Laboratory of
Johns Hopkins University. Among other things, he remarks:

". . . while I recognize the full importance of fundamental training in
the scientific discipline—namely the inculcation of habits of careful observation and critical reasoning, together with the acquisition of technical skill—
as essential for a research scientist, I do wish to emphasize that an alert
mind and a fertile and disciplined imagination are characteristics which are
absolutely indispensable to the scientist whose work is to rise above
mediocrity" (1953, p. 396).

Having familiarized ourselves with the physicists' concepts of science,
let us take a look at the recent trends in American archeology. According
to our new perspective, scientific laws cannot be proved, only disproved;
they may be statistical averages or they may describe no observable situation;
and they cannot be derived without the exercise of "disciplined imagination." After paying a visit to the realms of the incredible where physicists
are accustomed to spend much of their time, our wildest speculations about
the processes of culture look tame indeed, and we might even say sensible,
although this has ceased to be an adjective relevant to their truth. I do not
think anyone can deny that the cultural interpretations given in this volume
have a seductive simplicity, that they introduce a significant amount of
order into the chaotic jumble of facts unearthed and heaped up by the
archeologists. On the basis of the evidence just reviewed, we are obliged
to conclude that, whether or not their conclusions stand the test of time,
these synthesizers are proceeding in a scientific manner by applying to their
problems basic explanations of cultural phenomena.

These synthesizers are all archeologists. Since the subject of this series
is New World culture history, the significance of this fact is easily overlooked. It is only when we review current work in the general field of
anthropology that we become aware that archeologists have been quietly
assuming an increasingly important role in recent years. One measure of
this can be taken from an analysis of the fields represented by the officers
of the American Anthropological Association, who are listed in the front
of each issue of the *American Anthropologist*. The proportion of officers
who are archeologists averaged only $\frac{1}{8}$ to $\frac{1}{4}$ of the total in the five-year
period from 1945 to 1949, but in the five years since 1949 this figure has
risen to between $\frac{1}{3}$ and $\frac{1}{2}$. Since archeologists are greatly outnumbered by
ethnologists and social anthropologists, this rise is significant. It implies the

127

recognition of archeologists by their colleagues as anthropologists rather than as narrow specialists concerned only with recovering and preserving surviving remnants of the forgotten past.

This is a considerable achievement and represents a largely unconscious acknowledgment of the fact that American archeology has developed a "new look." The leading anthropologists of the past, from Tylor down to Boas and his students, were all primarily ethnologists or linguists. By the time archeology outgrew its antiquarian stage and began to develop special techniques to extract the maximum interpretative value from its data, ethnology was turning from material culture studies to psychological matters, and culture was being redefined as essentially a psychological phenomenon. From this point of view, archeological results were stigmatized as being hopelessly deficient and relegated to secondary importance. In a general anthropology text published as recently as 1949, such a view was expressed by a leading ethnologist:

"Archeology . . . is always limited in the results it can produce. It is doomed always to be the lesser part of anthropology. The use and meaning of any object depends almost wholly upon non-material behavior patterns, and the objects derive their true significance from such patterns. . . . Thus, when the archeologist uncovers a prehistoric culture, it is not really the culture that he unearths but merely the surviving products of that culture, tangible remains of the intangible reality. The actual culture became extinct when the society that carried it passed out of existence. No culture can exist divorced from living beings. . . ." (Hoebel, 1949, p. 436).

Although no explicit contradiction has been made, the actions and results of recent years indicate that archeologists are no longer convinced that they are inevitably doomed to being second-class anthropologists. Of basic significance in producing this change are the great strides that have been made in archeological interpretation. Refinements in the techniques of excavation, among them a more widespread application of the stratigraphic approach, and better methods of analysis, including numerical treatment of pottery types to give fine temporal distinctions and greater use of ethnographic parallels to fill out gaps in the non-material aspects of the extinct culture, have opened new vistas. The emergence of a radiocarbon method of absolute dating provides a more adequate basis for correlating cultural sequences in widely separated areas and thus determining not only relative speed of cultural development but direction of diffusion.

In making a break with the ethnology of the past, which gave rise to the basic theories of cultural evolution and diffusion, of culture areas and culture types, of the relation of culture to environment, and of culture as a superorganic phenomenon, modern ethnologists have left the way open to the archeologists to follow in the research paths opened by Tylor, Kroeber, Lowie, Wissler, and Boas. Fortified by their improved techniques, archeologists are beginning to show that they are singularly well equipped to take over this legacy. The strides that have been made in recent years indicate that far from being a handicap, there is a considerable advantage in being forced to deal with culture artificially separated from human beings. Shorn of the complicating and confusing psychological reactions of numbers of unique human personalities, cultural processes emerge in a stark and clear light. The remarkable accomplishment lies not with the archeologists who have recognized and profited by this advantage, but with those ethnologists like White (1949) who have been able to penetrate to fundamental cultural insights through the psychological maze.

American archeology has come of age. We have accumulated enough details about prehistoric cultures in most parts of the New World to begin drawing the kind of general conclusions that are contained in this volume. These results are of greater significance than the addition they make to our knowledge of New World prehistory. They offer a means of testing the cultural theories upon which anthropology is based, and archeologists are beginning to capitalize on this situation. It is a safe prediction that major contributions to cultural theory in the next few decades will be made by archeologists, whose laboratory encompasses the whole world and the whole history of culture.

If the possibility of achieving status for anthropology as a science with the prestige that physics now enjoys seems discouraging, it must be remembered that by comparison with physics, anthropology is very young. Newton's discoveries were made in the first part of the 18th century; those of Kepler and Galileo, 100 years earlier. Even if we consider that physics as a science begins with Newton, it is more than 200 years old. Before Newton are centuries of observation and explanation of natural phenomena, which although "unscientific" for the most part, formed a foundation for the emergence of physics as a science. Anthropology is frequently said to date from the middle of the 19th century, 150 years later than the latest date for the birth of physics and 250 years after Galileo and Kepler. When physics was 100 years old, the "atomic age" could not have been suspected. Anthropology is only 100 years old and exciting possibilities lie ahead. We know very little about them; but we can look forward with confidence in the knowledge that the science of culture will one day come into its own.

LITERATURE CITED

ALBRECHT, W. A.
   1943 Soil Fertility and the Human Species. Chemical and Engineering News, Vol. 22.
ANTEVS, ERNST
   1941 Age of the Cochise Culture Stages. Medallion Papers, No. 29, pp. 31-56. Gila Pueblo, Globe, Arizona.
BENNETT, WENDELL C.
   1946 The Archeology of the Central Andes. Handbook of South American Indians, Bureau of American Ethnology, Bulletin 143, Vol. 2, pp. 61-147.
BIRD, JUNIUS B.
   1948 Preceramic Changes in Chicama and Virú. Society for American Archeology, Memoir No. 4, pp. 21-28.
BOAS, FRANZ
   1895 Indians of British Columbia; Physical Characteristics. Report of the British Association for the Advancement of Science, pp. 522-592.
   1905 The Jesup North Pacific Expedition. 13th International Congress of Americanists, New York, 1902, pp. 91-100.
   1909 The Kwakiutl of Vancouver Island. American Museum of Natural History Memoirs, Vol. 8.
   1933 Relations between Northwest America and Northeast Asia. The American Aborigines, pp. 357-370. Toronto.
BORDEN, CHARLES E.
   1950 Preliminary Report on Archeological Investigations in the Fraser Delta Region. Anthropology in British Columbia, No. 1, pp. 13-27.
   1951 Facts and Problems of Northwest Coast Prehistory. Anthropology in British Columbia, No. 2, pp. 35-52.
   1954 Some Aspects of Prehistoric Coastal-Interior Relations in the Pacific Northwest. Anthropology in British Columbia, No. 4, pp. 26-31.
BRAINERD, GEORGE W.
   1951 Early Ceramic Horizons in Yucatan. Selected Papers of the 29th International Congress of Americanists, Vol. 1, The Civilizations of Ancient America, pp. 72-78.
   1953 A Cylindrical Stamp from Ecuador. The Masterkey, Vol. 27, No. 1. Los Angeles.
BUSHNELL, G. H. S.
   1951 The Archeology of the Santa Elena Peninsula in Southwest Ecuador. Cambridge University Press.
BUTLER, MARY
   1935 A Study of Maya Mouldmade Figurines. American Anthropologist, Vol. 37, pp. 636-672.
CARTER, GEORGE F.
   1950 Plant Evidence for Early Contacts with America. Southwestern Journal of Anthropology, Vol. 6, pp. 161-182.
CHILDE, V. GORDON
   1937 Man Makes Himself. Watts, London.
   1951 Social Evolution. London.

130

COLLINS, HENRY B., JR.
1937 Archeology of St. Lawrence Island. Smithsonian Institution Miscellaneous Collections, Vol. 96, No. 1.
1940 Outline of Eskimo Prehistory. Smithsonian Institution Miscellaneous Collections, Vol. 100, pp. 533-592.

COLTON, HAROLD S.
1938 Names of the Four Culture Roots in the Southwest. Science, Vol. 87, No. 2268.
1939 Prehistoric Culture Units and their Relationships in Northern Arizona. Museum of Northern Arizona Bul. 17. Flagstaff.

COTTER, JOHN L.
1954 Indications of a Paleo-Indian Co-Tradition for North America. American Antiquity, Vol. 20, pp. 64-67.

DAIFUKU, HIROSHI
1952 A New Conceptual Scheme for Prehistoric Cultures in the Southwestern United States. American Anthropologist, Vol. 54, pp. 191-201.

DALTON, O. M.
1897 Ethnographic Collections from the Northern Coast of North America. Archiv für Ethnologie, Vol. 10, pp. 227-245.

D'HARCOURT, M. R.
1947 Archéologie de la Province d'Esmeraldas, Equateur. Journal de la Société des Américanistes de Paris, Vol. 34, pp. 61-200.

DE LAGUNA, FREDERICA
1947 The Prehistory of Northern North America as Seen from the Yukon. Society for American Archeology, Memoir No. 3.

DICK, HERBERT W.
1952 Evidences of Early Man in Bat Cave and on the Plains of San Augustin, New Mexico. Selected Papers of the 29th International Congress of Americanists, Vol. 2, Indian Tribes of Aboriginal America, pp. 158-164.

DIESELDORF, E. P.
1926-1933 Kunst und Religion der Mayavolker. Berlin.

DI PESO, CHARLES C.
1953 The Sobaipuri Indians of the Upper San Pedro River Valley, Southeastern Arizona. Amerind Foundation Publ. No. 6. Dragoon, Arizona.

DIRAC, P. A. M.
1954 Quantum Mechanics and the Aether. The Scientific Monthly, Vol. 78, pp. 142-146.

DIXON, RONALD B.
1928 The Building of Cultures. New York.

DRUCKER, PHILIP
1939 Addenda on the Southwestern Ceremonial House. American Anthropologist, Vol. 41, pp. 644-647.
n. d. Field Notes from Tlingit, Haida, Niska, Tsimshian and Kwakiutl.

EDDINGTON, ARTHUR S.
1928 The Nature of the Physical World. Cambridge University Press.

EINSTEIN, ALBERT
1950 Out of my Later Years. Philosophical Library, New York.

EKHOLM, GORDON F.
1953 A Possible Focus of Asiatic Influence in the Late Classic Cultures of Mesoamerica. Society for American Archeology, Memoir No. 9, pp. 72-89.

ELLIS, BRUCE T.
1953 Vessel-lip Decoration as a Possible Guide to Southwestern Group Movements and Contacts. Southwestern Journal of Anthropology, Vol. 9, pp. 436-457.

EVANS, CLIFFORD AND BETTY J. MEGGERS
1950 Preliminary Results of Archeological Investigation at the Mouth of the Amazon. American Antiquity, Vol. 16, pp. 1-9.
n. d. British Guiana Field Notes, 1952-53.

GAMOW, GEORGE
1945 The Birth and Death of the Sun. Pelican Books.

131

GIBSON, R. E.
    1953 The Arts and Sciences. American Scientist, Vol. 41, pp. 389-409.
GIDDINGS, LOUIS
    1952 Ancient Bering Strait and Population Spread. Selected Papers of the Alaskan Science Conference.
GOETHALS, PETER R.
    ms. An Archeological Reconnaissance of Coastal Suriname. Master's Thesis on deposit at the Department of Anthropology, Yale University.
GOODSPEED, T. H., Editor
    1936 Essays in Geobotany in Honor of William Setchell. University of California Press.
GRIFFIN, JAMES B.
    1952 Some Early and Middle Woodland Pottery Types in Illinois. Hopewellian Communities in Illinois, Thorne Deuel, Editor, Illinois State Museum Scientific Papers, pp. 93-130. Springfield.
GRIFFIN, JAMES B. AND ALEX D. KRIEGER
    1947 Notes on Some Ceramic Techniques and Intrusions in Central Mexico. American Antiquity, Vol. 12, pp. 156-168.
HALL, EDWARD T. AND GEORGE L. TRAGER
    1953 The Analysis of Culture. American Council of Learned Societies, Washington, D.C.
HAURY, EMIL W.
    1953 Artifacts with the Mammoth Remains, Naco, Arizona. American Antiquity, Vol. 19, pp. 1-25.
HAURY, EMIL W. AND OTHERS
    1950 The Stratigraphy and Archeology of Ventana Cave, Arizona. University of Arizona and University of New Mexico Press.
HEINE-GELDERN, ROBERT AND GORDON F. EKHOLM
    1951 Significant Parallels in the Symbolic Arts of Southern Asia and Middle America. Selected Papers, 29th International Congress of Americanists, Vol. 1, The Civilizations of Ancient America, pp. 299-309.
HEIZER, R. F.
    1943 Aconite Poison Whaling in Asia and America: an Aleutian Transfer to the New World. Bureau of American Ethnology Bulletin 133, pp. 415-468.
HERSKOVITS, MELVILLE J.
    1948 Man and his Works. New York.
HEYL, PAUL R.
    1954 Space, Time and Einstein (1928). Reprinted in A Treasury of Science, Harlow Shapley, Editor, pp. 269-275. New York.
HOEBEL, E. A.
    1949 Man in the Primitive World: an Introduction to Anthropology. New York.
HUTCHINSON, J. B., R. A. SILOW AND S. G. STEPHENS
    1947 The Evolution of Gassypium. Oxford University Press.
JEANS, JAMES
    1943 Physics and Philosophy. Cambridge University Press.
JOHNSON, FRED, Editor
    1951 Radiocarbon Dating. Society for American Archeology, Memoir No. 8.
KIDDER, ALFRED V.
    1927 Southwestern Archaeological Conference. Science, n. s., Vol. 66, No. 1716, pp. 489-491.
KING, ARDEN R.
    1948 Tripod Pottery in the Central Andean Area. American Antiquity, Vol. 14, pp. 103-115.
KIRCHOFF, PAUL
    1943 Mesoamerica. Acta Americana, Vol. 1, pp. 92-107.
KROEBER, ALFRED L.
    1923 American Culture and the Northwest Coast. American Anthropologist, Vol. 25, pp. 1-20.
    1930 Cultural Relations between North and South America. 23rd International Congress of Americanists, New York, 1928, pp. 5-22.

1939 Cultural and Natural Areas of Native North America. University of California Publications in American Archeology and Ethnology, Vol. 38.

1948a Anthropology: Race, Language, Culture, Psychology, Prehistory. New York.

1948b Summary and Interpretations. Society for American Archeology, Memoir No. 4, pp. 113-121.

LANTIS, MARGARET

1938 The Alaskan Whale-cult and its Affinities. American Anthropologist, Vol. 40, pp. 438-464.

1947 Alaskan Eskimo Ceremonialism. American Ethnological Society Monograph, Vol. 11.

LARSEN, HELGE AND FROELICH RAINEY

1948 Ipiutak and the Arctic Whaling Culture. American Museum of Natural History, Anthropological Papers, Vol. 42.

LAUGHLIN, W. S.

1952a Contemporary Problems in the Anthropology of Southeastern Alaska. Arctic Institute of America Publication, Science in Alaska, pp. 66-84.

1952b The Aleut-Eskimo Community. University of Alaska Anthropological Papers, Vol. 1, pp. 25-46.

LEHMANN, HENRI

1951 Le Personnage Couché sur le Dos: Commun dans l'Archéologie du Mexique et de l'Equateur. Selected Papers, 29th International Congress of Americanists, Vol. 1, The Civilizations of Ancient America, pp. 291-298.

LIANG, S. Y.

1930 New Stone Age Pottery from the Prehistoric Site at Hsi-Yin Tsun, Shansi China. American Anthropological Association Memoir 37.

LOTHROP, SAMUEL K.

1936 Zacualpa, a Study of Ancient Quiché Artifacts. Carnegie Institution of Washington, Publication 472.

1942 Coclé, an Archeological Study of Central Panama. Peabody Museum of American Archeology and Ethnology Memoirs, Vol. 8.

1951 Peruvian Metallurgy. Selected Papers, 29th International Congress of Americanists, Vol. 1, The Civilizations of Ancient America, pp. 219-223.

MACNEISH, RICHARD S.

1950 A Synopsis of the Archaeological Sequence in the Sierra de Tamaulipas. Revista Mexicana de Estudios Antropologicos, Vol. 11, pp. 79-96.

MANGELSDORF, PAUL C. AND C. E. SMITH, JR.

1949 New Archaeological Evidence on Evolution in Maize. Botanical Museum Leaflet, Vol. 13, No. 8 Harvard University.

MARTIN, PAUL S. AND JOHN B. RINALDO

1951 The Southwestern Co-Tradition. Southwestern Journal of Anthropology, Vol. 7, pp. 215-230.

MARTIN, PAUL S., JOHN B. RINALDO AND OTHERS

1952 Mogollon Cultural Continuity and Change, the Stratigraphic Analysis of Tularosa and Cordova Caves. Fieldiana: Anthropology, Vol. 40. Chicago Natural History Museum.

McGREGOR, JOHN C.

1941 Winona and Ridge Ruin. Museum of Northern Arizona Bulletin 18.

MEGGERS, BETTY J.

1954 Environmental Limitation on the Development of Culture. American Anthropologist, Vol. 56. pp. 801-824.

MEGGERS, BETTY J. AND CLIFFORD EVANS

ms. Archeological Investigations at the Mouth of the Amazon. To be published in one of the anthropological series of the Smithsonian Institution.

MERA, H. P.

1934 Observations on the Archeology of the Petrified Forest National Monument. Laboratory of Anthropology, Technical Series, Bulletin 7. Santa Fe.

MORRIS, EARL H.

1927 The Beginnings of Pottery Making in the San Juan Area: Unfired Prototypes and the Wares of the Earliest Ceramic Period. American Museum of Natural History, Anthropological Papers, Vol. 28, pt. 2.

PORTER, MURIEL NOÉ
1953 Tlatilco and the Pre-Classic Cultures of the New World. Viking Fund Publications in Anthropology, No. 19.
READ, C. H.
1891 Account of a Collection . . . Journal of the Royal Anthropological Institute, Vol. 21, pp. 99-108.
REICHEL-DOLMATOFF, GERARDO
1954 A Preliminary Study of Space and Time Perspective in Northern Colombia. American Antiquity, Vol. 19, pp. 352-366.
REICHENBACH, HANS
1942 From Copernicus to Einstein. Philosophical Library, New York.
ROBERTS, FRANK H. H., JR.
1935 A Survey of Southwestern Archeology. American Anthropologist, Vol. 37, pp. 1-35.
RUDY, JACK R. AND ROBERT D. STIRLAND
1950 An Archeological Reconnaissance in Washington County, Utah. University of Utah, Department of Anthropology, Anthropological Papers, No. 9.
SAPIR, EDWARD
1916 Time Perspective in Aboriginal American Culture, a Study in Method. Canada Department of Mines, Geological Survey, Memoir 90. Ottawa.
SCHROEDER, ALBERT H.
1947 Did the Sinagua of the Verde Valley Settle in the Salt River Valley? Southwestern Journal of Anthropology, Vol. 3, pp. 230-246.
SILLMAN, LEONARD
1953 The Genesis of Man. International Journal of Psychoanalysis, Vol. 34.
SILOW, R. A.
1953 The Problems of Trans-Pacific Migration Involved in the Origin of the Cultivated Cottons of the New World. Proceedings 7th Pacific Science Congress, New Zealand, 1945, Vol. 5, pp. 112-118.
SIMPSON, C. G.
1947 Holarctic Mammalian Faunas and Continental Relationships during the Cenozoic. Bulletin of the Geological Society of America, Vol. 58.
SMITH, C. E., JR.
1950 Prehistoric Plant Remains from Bat Cave. Botanical Museum Leaflet, Vol. 14, No. 7. Harvard University.
SMITH, HARLAN I.
1907 Archaeology of the Gulf of Georgia and Puget Sound. American Museum of Natural History, Memoir 4, pp. 303-441.
1909 Shell-heaps of the Lower Fraser. American Museum of Natural History, Memoir 4, pp. 133-191.
SPINDEN, HERBERT J.
1917 The Origin and Distribution of Agriculture in America. 19th International Congress of Americanists, Washington, 1915, pp. 269-276.
STEWARD, JULIAN H.
1948 Culture Areas of the Tropical Forest. Handbook of South American Indians, Bureau of American Ethnology, Bulletin 143, Vol. 3, pp. 883-899.
1949a South American Cultures: an Interpretative Summary. Handbook of South American Indians, Bureau of American Ethnology, Bulletin 143, Vol. 5, pp. 669-772.
1949b Cultural Causality and Law: a Trial Formulation of the Development of Early Civilization. American Anthropologist, Vol. 51, pp. 1-27.
STEWARD, JULIAN, Editor
1946-1950 Handbook of South American Indians. Bureau of American Ethnology, Bulletin 143, Vols. 1-6.
STRONG, WILLIAM DUNCAN
1927 An Analysis of Southwestern Society. American Anthropologist, Vol. 29, pp. 1-61.
1943 Cross-Sections of New World Prehistory. Smithsonian Miscellaneous Collections, Vol. 104, No. 2.

134

STRONG, WILLIAM DUNCAN AND CLIFFORD EVANS
    1952 Cultural Stratigraphy in the Virú Valley, Northern Peru. Columbia Studies in Archeology and Ethnology, Vol. 4. Columbia University Press.
SULLIVAN, J. W. N.
    1933 The Limitations of Science. Viking Press, New York.
SWADESH, MORRIS
    1950 Salish Internal Relationships. International Journal of American Linguistics, Vol. 16, pp. 157-167.
    1952a Lexico-Statistical Dating of Prehistoric Ethnic Contacts with Special Reference to North American Indians and Eskimos. American Philosophical Society Proceedings, Vol. 96, No. 4, pp. 452-463.
    1952b Review of Shafer, 1952. International Journal of American Linguistics, Vol. 18, pp. 178-181.
TOULOUSE, JOSEPH H., JR.
    1949 The Mission of San Gregorio de Abó: a Report of the Excavation and Repair of a Seventeenth Century New Mexico Mission. Monograph of the School of American Research, No. 13, Santa Fe.
TRAGER, GEORGE L.
    1951 Linguistic History and Ethnologic History in the Southwest. Journal of the Washington Academy of Sciences, Vol. 41, pp. 341-343.
WAGLEY, CHARLES
    1953 Amazon Town, a Study of Man in the Tropics. Macmillan, New York.
WAUCHOPE, ROBERT
    1950 A Tentative Sequence of Pre-Classic Ceramics in Middle America. Middle American Research Records, Vol. 1, No. 14, Tulane University.
    1954 Implications of Radiocarbon Dates from Middle and South America. Middle American Research Records, Vol. 2, No. 2, Tulane University.
WEDEL, WALDO R.
    1953 Some Aspects of Human Ecology in the Central Plains. American Anthropologist, Vol. 55, pp. 499-514.
WENDORF, FRED
    1953 Salvage Archaeology in the Chama Valley, New Mexico. Monographs of the School of American Research, No. 17. Santa Fe.
WHITE, LESLIE A.
    1949 The Science of Culture. Farrar, Straus, New York.
WILLEY, GORDON R.
    1949 Ceramics. Handbook of South American Indians, Bureau of American Ethnology Bulletin 143, Vol. 5, pp. 139-204.
WORMINGTON, H. M.
    1953 Origins, Indigenous Period. Program of the History of America, Vol. I, No. 1. Instituto Panamericano de Geografia y Historia. Mexico.

DATE DUE

APR 2 2 '78			
DEC 7 1981			
MAY 2 9 2009			
GAYLORD			PRINTED IN U.S.A.